THE POET'S TOMB

Illuminations: A Series on American Poetics

Series Editor: Jon Thompson

Illuminations focuses on the poetics and poetic practices of the contemporary moment in the USA. The series is particularly keen to promote a set of reflective works that include, but go beyond, traditional academic prose, so we take Walter Benjamin's rich, poetic essays published under the title of *Illuminations* as an example of the kind of approach we most value. Collectively, the titles published in this series aim to engage various audiences in a dialogue that will reimagine the field of contemporary American poetics. For more about the series, please visit its website at parlorpress.com/illuminations.

Books in the Series

The Poet's Tomb: The Material Soul of Poetry by Martin Corless-Smith
Vestiges: Notes, Responses, and Essays 1988–2018 by Eric Pankey
Sudden Eden by Donald Revell
Prose Poetry and the City by Donna Stonecipher

THE POET'S TOMB

THE MATERIAL SOUL OF POETRY

Martin Corless-Smith

Parlor Press
Anderson, South Carolina
www.parlorpress.com

Parlor Press LLC, Anderson, South Carolina, USA
© 2021 by Parlor Press
Printed in the United States of America on acid-free paper.
  SAN: 2 5 4 - 8 8 7 9

                Library of Congress Cataloging-in-Publication Data

Names: Corless-Smith, Martin, author.
Title: The poet's tomb : the material soul of poetry / Martin Corless-Smith.
Description: Anderson, South Carolina : Parlor Press, [2021] | Series: Illumi-
    nations: a series on American poetics | Includes bibliographical references. |
    Summary: "Tracks the evolution of consciousness as defined by and contained
    in poetry from the Ancient to the Contemporary. Using the work of Sappho,
    Virgil, Keats, Celan, and Alice Notley, the book argues for a material founda-
    tion for consciousness and ideas such as the Sublime and the Soul"-- Provided
    by publisher.
Identifiers: LCCN 2021026606 (print) | LCCN 2021026607 (ebook) | ISBN
    9781643171760 (paperback) | ISBN 9781643171777 (pdf) | ISBN
    9781643171784 (epub)
Subjects: LCSH: Poetics--Philosophy. | Philosophical anthropology in literature.
Classification: LCC PN1077 .C67 2021 (print) | LCC PN1077 (ebook) | DDC
    809.1/9384--dc23
LC record available at https://lccn.loc.gov/2021026606
LC ebook record available at https://lccn.loc.gov/2021026607

978-1-64317-176-0 (paperback)
978-1-64317-177-7 (pdf)
978-1-64317-178-4 (epub)

Illuminations: A Series on American Poetics
Series Editor: Jon Thompson

Cover art: "The Grotto of Posillipo at Naples"by Antonie Sminck Pitloo.
    1826. Oil on canvas. Rijksmuseum, Amsterdam, Netherlands. Public
    domain: http://hdl.handle.net/10934/RM0001.COLLECT.5465
Interior and cover design: David Blakesley

Parlor Press, LLC is an independent publisher of scholarly and trade titles in print
and multimedia formats. This book is available in paper, cloth and eBook formats from Parlor Press on the World Wide Web at http://www.parlorpress.com or
through online and brick-and-mortar bookstores. For submission information or
to find out about Parlor Press publications, write to Parlor Press, 3015 Bracken-
berry Drive, Anderson, South Carolina, 29621, or email editor@parlorpress.com.

Contents

Introduction: The Poem's Soul

These essays have as their focus a few mostly well-known poems by a few mostly famous poets (with a few philosophical texts, a novel, a memoir and artworks employed here and there), but my main concern really is with being, and in particular with the uncanny role that poems play in the history of consciousness, in making it and mapping it. Perhaps in the end what I am interested in doing is sketching some shadows of the soul, glimpsed in passing, and I see the poem as the greatest mirror of that particular invisibility. My readings are subject to diversions and eddies (because to a certain degree real poems resist reading), but I hope that in trying to read the works included here, and in following their leads, it becomes clear that I am examining and exhibiting the ways in which reading a poem is an interactive exchange of extraordinary productivity, drawing the reader into the ongoing spectacle of the history of being. Reading is a flourishing communion of sorts. A single line is seed to a forest. These essays are all born from such fertile roots. The fuss and tangles in my essays are evidence of my errant husbandry, of my being, of my having been.

It might be argued that any history of poetry is also a history of the soul's development, and that the important metaphors in great poems give us the ways and means of understanding our own being[1]. Reading a poem is an investment of faith, a giving over. It is in this giving over that we encounter ourselves in otherness, as otherness. Without this thorough encounter of language, without reading poems, we easily slip back into a docile, inarticulate performance of being. Without the efforts of working through a poem's difficulty, we do not cross the near and far of being.

And we never finish reading until we finish being. These essays are partial readings, and as such, they are trials with incomplete judgments, efforts, tangents: three tries and out. If there is any truth, it lies in their erring.

---

1. The meaning of "soul" is obviously a moot point here. The same is true for *poetry*.

The prologue examines Anne Carson's *Eros the Bitter-sweet*, and sets up a proposal of poetry as an originating event of human self-consciousness: Sappho's word *bittersweet* is read as an exemplary site where exclusive elements are held in combination. This becomes our first model of consciousness.

In Leopardi's *L'infinito* I try to show the mind and body of poetry, in poetry, using the tiny "infinity" as a key for unlocking his ideas of the soul in his epic *Zibaldone*.

The central essay of the book is a romp through the grave matter of poets and their tombs. Starting with Virgil's epitaph, the essay shows a development of variations on the poem as memorial. It ends up with Alice Notley undoing Virgil, tearing up the monument, and turning all the ghosts loose.

Finally, I read Herrick's *Hesperides* as a poetic Arcady, an English garden planted with every heirloom seed nurtured to various golden fruits. Like Sappho's *bittersweet*, the paradoxical *"wild civility"* of Herrick's poems provide the necessary frisson of self and other that opens out into the space of consciousness: the playful arena of his great book is itself an assertion and articulation of poetry as a realm of being.

The stakes for addressing the soul in poetry might seem esoteric and even indulgently irrelevant given today's ugly political climate, and the anxieties abounding with regard to climate and culture. But a reading of poetry is hopefully instructive, and a focus on its connection to self seems always timely. Any description of the soul is not merely a metaphorical distraction, it is a definitive articulation of the most profound political ground of all: selfhood.

My predominantly materialist view does not dispense with "soul" as some ethereal fantasy, it hopes to see that the physical and material is where the phenomenon of being is encountered, much like Spinoza argues in his *Ethics*. The printed body of a poem houses the phenomenon of its powerful and spell-binding authority: Poetry, the loftiest of human endeavors, always comes back to the body.

And not just to the body of the poet (a central concern for these essays). The poem is not simply a preservation of individuality (is there such a thing?), or even individual talent (though it is evidence of that), it is an offering of community, of something essential beyond the individual. Just as the self does not bask in isolated *sui generis* glory, but opens up only in exchange, I see the poem as a common ground, as an alternative body or *house of being* where we might, as with another person, encounter evidence of thought and memory.

When we face a poem, when we agree to read and listen, we are accepting it as a voiced, willed otherness, rather than just mere words (even if that *voice* remains abstract or unintelligible, if it is a poem it must carry the aura of human intent). And we engage with a poem in ways similar to the ways we engage with other people. Through language, our common ground, we acknowledge the stranger, listen for tone, gauge intent, and as with other people, we notice our differences— we try to access that which at first seems intractable, to learn its meaning, to understand something of its essence. And in so doing we learn to become human. We slowly make up a self only in this way.

Reading a poem is not a surrogate for other human interactions, but it is party to them. The central purpose of reading poetry is not to elect a canon, (though in an historical/political world dominated by such practices that has become the common approach) but to engage intimately with otherness. We might see this engagement as a battle of wits, a performance of aesthetics, a gift of truth, an exchange of love, or as a witnessing of history; but above all those, we might see it as a, or even *the*, model activity of being human. And that thing that we recognize in the face of another, that very essential attribute that plays over the features that we call *soul*, there is a similar phenomenon that enlivens the words of a poem, something that allows us to read them as humanly significant. And we might call that uncanny presence of the human, carried in the words of the poem, *Poetry*[2].

---

2. Early in his *Biographia Literaria*, Coleridge suggests that "[o]ur genuine admiration of a great poet is a continuous under-current of feeling; it is everywhere present, but seldom anywhere as a separate excitement." His description of this under-current bears reference to contemporary descriptions of the relation between mind and brain.

Acknowledgments

"Living on the Edge, the Bittersweet Place of Poetry" appeared in *Anne Carson: Ecstatic Lyre (Under Discussion)*, edited by Joshua Marie Wilkinson, University of Michigan Press, 2015.

"Leopardi's Material Infinite" appeared in *Denver Quarterly*, Spring 2019.

"Herrick's Wild Civility" appeared in *The Ben Jonson Journal*, 20.2, 2013 University of Edinburgh Press.

"On Sublimity" appeared in *Evening Will Come: A Monthly Journal of Poetics* 6, June 2011. http://www.thevolta.org/ewc6-mcorless-smith-p1.html

---

The phenomenon we call mind requires the body of the brain, of that we are sure, but our current physics does not supply us with the necessary understanding to know how such material manifests the operations of thought.

The raving mouth—or why the muse ain't moribund

According to Heraclitus, the Sybil, with ranting mouth, utters things without humour, without adornment, without perfume, and yet, thanks to god, she reaches down a thousand years with her voice.

—Plutarch
On the Failure of the Oracle of Delphi These Days to use Verse

Do you not see with what grace Sappho's verses charm and seduce the hearer? But the Sybil, with raving mouth, according to Heraclitus, speaking without mirth, or adornment or perfume, traverses with her voice a thousand years with the help of god.

—Plutarch
Why the Pythia No Longer Prophesies in Verse

The Sybil, according to Heraclitus, speaks truths that last a thousand years: unadulterated—and as Plutarch notes—not seductive like the lyrics of Sappho. But, god-given, inspired—raving with en-theos-iasm—The Word is divine prophecy.

We know the Sybil speaks in riddles. She is φωνή becoming λόγος, the voice (phoné) becoming word (logos)—the instant that Agamben describes as "the momentary god". All words that become meaningful were raved from the gift of tongues.

The arrival of the logos is exosomatic. When our voice bears sense it is a gift of meaning immediately other to ourselves (in order for it to be communicable). This is the instant of the anthropogenesis—birth of the Homo Sapien Loquendi. This is the space of consciousness.

By Badiou's reckoning, this moment is the meeting of the matheme with the phoneme. It is where Philosophy (as knowledge) meets Poetry (as venture).

When the Sybil raves she births knowledge from a rant. In this regard she is living poetry.

Where does the new word come from? The new metaphor—the new moment of divinity? It is called the gift of the muse—it is museic—it is closer to song than to knowledge. We call upon the muse because we alone cannot be the source of new knowledge. We must ask for words beyond our knowledge. These are all metaphors.

We read the metaphors because we believe they have meaning. They last as long as we are reading them. We believed in the gift and this was their truth. Poetry makes reading necessary. To become knowledge it must be read with the faith of one seeking divine truth.

Poetry seeks truth through the divine gift of raving: the chance for voice to make meaning. Ranting and reading.

Poetry, in its venturing, is brave—because what is spoken is ecstatic beyond self, and that is tantamount to death.

Death makes us human. And so does poetry.

(For Notley the muse is a dead woman, because death and poetry are both immortal counterparts to our mortality).

Works Not Cited

Agamben, Giorgio. *What Is Philosophy?*
Badiou, Alain. *The Age of the Poets.*
Barnes, Jonathan. *Early Greek Philosophy*
Waterfield, Robin. *The First Philosophers*

THE POET'S TOMB

Prologue: Living on the Edge, the Bittersweet Place of Poetry.

When I was offered the chance to write on Carson's *Eros the Bittersweet* I worried that I had read it insufficiently, that my relationship with it was at best tangential—in fact I worried that the whole scape of my reading was entirely too unruly and determined by extraneous factors and extravagant detours that had no true bearing on the text being offered. My reading dilemma was not particular to Carson's text of course, but in the end it did seem a problem the book itself might acknowledge to some degree (even if in the end the book does try to settle into a conclusive shape). Reading any book entails much of the erotic reaching that forms the central concern of Carson's volume.

Reading, like loving is a bittersweet endeavor.

Eros the Bittersweet is a book of readings, of links between disparate texts that tries to perpetuate and support a developing theme. It examines the erotic crisis as exemplified by Sappho's neologism *glukupikron*,[1] the *bittersweet* of the title. It becomes apparent that the term's affective tension comes from the inherent paradox of its juxtaposing simultaneous opposing feelings (sensations, or tastes), and that it is the frisson of the simultaneity of these dissonant counterparts that is Carson's essential investigation.

---

1. Translated by Carson originally as *sweetbitter*, an attempt to mimic the progression from sweetness to bitter in the Greek original.

3

In his book *Erotism* Georges Bataille describes the Erotic crisis as the defining instance of selfhood[2]. Bataille characterizes the state of the self-conscious individual as "discontinuous", that is, separate from everything else, from the "continuity."

We are discontinuous beings, individuals who perish in isolation in the midst of an incomprehensible adventure, but we yearn for our lost continuity.[3]

That continuity is the ground from which our individuality is rent. Returning to that continuity spells an end to selfhood:

Continuity is what we are after, but generally only if that continuity which the death of discontinuous beings can also establish is not the victor in the long run. What we desire is to bring into a world founded on discontinuity all the continuity such a world can sustain...For the man in love . . . love may be felt violently. . . . We ought never forget that in spite of the bliss love promises its first effect is one of turmoil and distress. . . . Its essence is to substitute for the persistent discontinuity a miraculous continuity between two beings.[4]

Entering or re-entering this continuity would require a fusion with otherness that would end our individuality. We could never experience continuity as our selves.

Hence love spells suffering for us in so far as it is a quest for the impossible[5].

The structure of Erotic crisis is not limited to the model of the frustrated desires of a lover (although this is the preeminent example in Carson). It is the crisis of being in general.[6] According to Bataille:

---

2. "As Sokrates tells it, your story begins the moment Eros enters you." Carson, 152.

3. Bataille, Georges, *Erotism: Death and Sensuality* (San Francisco: City Lights, 1986), 15.

4. Bataille, 18-19.

5. Bataille, 20

6. The structure of this schism as the foundational event of consciousness bears a striking resemblance to Lacan's Mirror Stage, and to Freudian models of the birth of identity that Carson refers to later.

Man achieves his inner experience at the instant when bursting out of the chrysalis he feels that he is tearing himself, not tearing something outside that resists him.[7]

Carson describes this as "the moment the soul parts on itself"[8]. Man is not an object ripped from the mould of nature, Man's consciousness *is* the rip. Man stands abashed before Love and Death, those catastrophic events that offer to heal the wound of his isolation, yet simultaneously to overwhelm and annihilate. This is the erotic crisis housed in Sappho's neologism, the bitter sweet paradox of Carson's title.

The event of this crisis is also where we might find Heidegger's description of the Poet lurking. Bataille's *continuity* is markedly similar to Heidegger's *Open* (which he himself finds in Rilke). The term denotes all that which is beyond the limits of the discontinuous self. It is the task of the Poet to push into the Open.

The higher its consciousness, the more the conscious being is excluded from the world. This is why man, in the words of Rilke's letter, is "before the world." He is not admitted into the Open. Man stands over against the world.[9]

Plants and animals "do not will because, muted in their desire, they never bring the Open before themselves as an object."[10] Thus it is man alone whose "desire" places him before the Open. Heidegger names this willing *venturesomeness*. The poet is that being who ventures, turning towards the Open. The poet's being is directed toward the continuity, in the same way a lover's is towards the beloved. The poet's "being" is marked by the word:

Language is the precinct (templum), that is, the house of Being ... [poets] dare the precinct of Being. They dare language.[11]

---

7. Bataille, 39

8. Carson, 7

9. Heidegger, Martin "What Are Poets for" *Poetry, Language, Thought*, 106

10. Ibid., 108

11. Ibid., 129

Or as Carson puts it: "Eros is the ground where logos takes root between two people."[12] Much of her book examines edges and borders, and that uncanny space between self and other, whether that be between lovers or between reader and writer. Both lovers and readers and writers are motivated by erotic desire. What seems different though is the presence of the text.

When I started to read Carson I was disturbed by a strange but increasingly dwelt upon metaphorical slip, as I saw it. A movement from a split to a triangulation.

In describing the action of metaphor, that which like *bittersweet* itself, brings "two heterogeneous things close to reveal their closeness,"[13] Carson enumerates the effects as "triangulates, haunts, splits, wrenches and delights." Notice two making three. So let us look at the metaphors Carson uses to illuminate the instant of the erotic split.

Sweetbitter eros is what hits the raw film of the lover's mind. Paradox is what takes shape on the sensitized plate of the poem, a negative image from which positive pictures can be created.[14]

Here we have the rip of consciousness described as film. One sees the rupture of consciousness, if you like, in the act of peeling the polaroid negative off its positive, so that we have both sides of a desired union reft apart in the forging of the image of that desire. But it seems a step removed somehow to have this rupture projected upon the raw film of the lover's mind. Somehow the rupture has produced an image that is now projected. The polaroid is immediate, the film projection requires a secondary step.

If the erotic act of desiring is itself the act that causes the consciousness of the rupture. The ego's arousal marks the division of self and other by its very action.

---

12. Carson, 145

13. Ibid., 73

14. Carson, 9

What happens next is the ongoing project of the ego. In short, the split becomes itself a realm of investment. Someone looks at the polaroid (someone took it).

The schism between lover and beloved or the *discontinuous* and the *continuity*, a whole broken into two, now becomes three. It is the worrying of two into three that plays throughout Carson's book.

In his critique of Heidegger's portrayal of Holderlin, Hans-Jost Frey looks at exactly this worrying of a duality into a tri-angulation.[15] In particular Frey is concerned about Heidegger dragging the semantic meaning of the poem onto the event of its making.

The general essence of poetry . . . is equally valid for all poetry [not just work such as Holderlin's which chooses as its subject the writing of poetry] . . .Writing the essence of poetry does not mean expressing it.[16]

If for Heidegger "the word is the occurrence of the sacred"[17] Frey wants to make sure we realize that the "sacred does not exist in the word by being named but by happening with it."[18] For Heidegger "song is not just mankind's work. Something is also not the work of god, who is dependent on Mankind. Song therefore testifies neither to mankind nor to God but to their inseparability. In this case the song (or poem) is the ground upon which the erotic catastrophe is enacted. But, this is (if we choose to agree) song's ontology, not its semantics. "The word that names the sacred is not itself sacred."[19] It is however, the occurrence of the sacred.

If the poem is not what it expresses insofar as it expresses what it is, then this does not mean that it can't be what it expresses. It only means that it is

---

15. Frey, Hans-Jost, *Studies in Poetic Discourse: Mallarmé, Baudelaire, Rimbaud, Hölderlin* (Stanford: Stanford University Press, 1996).

16. Ibid., 178

17. Ibid., 180

18. Ibid., 180

19. Ibid., 183

not by making itself the object of its own discourse that the poem is what it expresses.[20]

Frey argues that Heidegger conflates these two states, "the expressed event for the event of expression" whereas Holderlin is careful to distinguish them:

The immediate ubiquity is the mediation for everything conveyed, that is for the mediate. The immediate is itself never a mediate, although the immediate is strictly speaking, the mediation, that is, the mediateness of the mediate, because it enables it with its own essence.[21]

The poem is the event of the reach from the discontinuous poet towards continuity. According to Frey the proposition of a poem is a mediation that might discuss its mediation, but the discussion as such neither helps nor hinders its task. But this does not seem to allow the poem to function as anything more than an instant of language. Frey sees the poem as a significant event but importantly not as an event of signification. It seems in separating the two events he believes Heidegger conflates he has not kept the two as necessary counterparts in the poetic act. The poem in its mediation marks the realm of the necessary link between self and other. Nature (for Holderlin), The Open (for Rilke or Heidegger) or the continuity (for Bataille) is the realm within which the poem articulates its separation from Nature et al, "as the unmediated enabling of all mediation, nature is the immediate."[22] Or as Carson puts it: "Eros is the ground where logos takes root between two people."[23] But why should a poem be important for this job, more so than a simple sentence?

In discussing Sappho's most enduring lyric, Fragment 31, Carson discovers a "ruse" whereby Sappho interposes a male viewer for her beloved. This "triangulation" offers an allegorical model of the structure "for, where is eros is lack, its activation

---

20. Ibid., 184
21. Ibid., 188
22. Ibid., 189
23. Carson, 145

MARTIN CORLESS-SMITH

8

calls for three structural components—lover, beloved and that which comes between them."[24] Continuing her film metaphor Carson imagines: "the ideal is projected on a screen of the actual, in a kind of stereoscopy. "[25] This layering of the structure of the erotic split with the observation of its enactment is exactly the conflation Frey points out in Heidegger. But Carson does not conflate, she understands the necessity of the "ruse:"[26]

A space must be maintained or desire ends. Sappho reconstructs the space of desire in a poem that is like a small, perfect photograph of the erotic dilemma.[27]

This is a significant space, for it marks the arena where self comes into being. According to Bruno Snell, Sappho's split adjective *glukupikron* is the actual historical instant where the Greeks invent self-consciousness. It is the instant of the maintained schism that produces the ground upon which consciousness can be projected. Metaphor, and thinking work "by projecting sameness upon difference." Bittersweet manages the deliberate ruse of meaning two incompatibilities. We read it as an intentional impossibility. It itself describes *and* enacts the erotic dilemma. It maintains the space of desire (albeit a small space between syllables). In a way we could describe this one word as a poem of sorts. This task is particular to poetry in that it houses blatant paradoxes that are both read and resist reading. Poetry revels in such frissons.

The self forms at the edge of desire[28]. The task of the poem is to perform these edges that signify their reaching out into the Open.

The poet, in reveling at (or in) the edge between self and other (in using language), in enacting a mediation, cannot rest in this mediation as if now unified with otherness, she can only offer the instant up as one of reaching. The poem is an indi-

---

24. Carson, 16

25. Ibid., 16

26. "To know both, keeping the difference visible is the subterfuge called eros." Carson, .69

27. Ibid., 26

28. Ibid., 39

cation of the event of self-consciousness that enacts the occurrence of self in relation to otherness.

The semantic meaning of the poem is not identical to the ontological event of the poem, but it does seem that some special frisson, or mise-en-abyme occurs if the subject matter interacts with the functional event of the writing. If poetic language leans towards presence, if this is the open topic of its articulation, we gain as a reader both the mediation which is the house of self consciousness, and the drama of that self-consciousness, the signification of which seems significant.

Carson's *Eros the Bittersweet*, reads the event of the poetic metaphor as the realm of the imagination:

> *The innovation of metaphor occurs in . . . [its] shift of distance from far to near, and it is effected by imagination. A virtuoso act of imagination [such as Sappho's neologism bittersweet] brings the two things together, sees their incongruence, then sees also a new congruence, meanwhile continuing to recognize the previous incongruence through the new congruence.*[29]

Carson argues that metaphor is the shape of thinking, the consciousness of being. The unprecedented effect of language is to provide a provisional realm where consciousness enacts its awareness, along with its desire to house that consciousness more permanently in the world. The drama of being is to come into the joy of acknowledging selfhood by an event that causes that self to be held adrift. Poems seem to be then, both the event, and the drama of that event acknowledged:

> *The construction of poems becomes the record of a series of individual thresholds of the experience of being conscious; they form the definitions, in time and in language, of human identity.*[30]

The significance of Sappho's poem is not merely that it provides an historical marker as perhaps the first acknowledgement of the ontological structure of poetry, it is simultaneous-

---

29. Carson, 73

30. Forrest-Thomson, Veronica, *Collected Poems and Translations*, 263

ly the event of consciousness opening the fragile arena where selfhood and otherness perform. As Carson has it, Poetry is the self-conscious event of human consciousness *par excellence*.

Works Cited

Bataille, Georges. *Erotism: Death and Sensuality*. San Francisco: City Lights, 1986.

Carson, Anne. *Eros the Bittersweet*. McLean, IL: Dalkey Archive Press, 1998.

Frey, Hans-Jost. *Studies in Poetic Discourse: Mallarmé, Baudelaire, Rimbaud, Hölderlin*. Stanford: Stanford University Press, 1996.

Forrest-Thomson, Veronica. *Collected Poems and Translations*. Lewes, UK: Allardyce Barnett, 1990.

Heidegger, Martin. *Poetry, Language, Thought*. New York: Harper Colophon, 1975

By Giovanni Bellini - National Gallery, London, Public Domain, https://commons.wikimedia.org/w/index.php?curid=85107.

1 Leopardi's Material Infinite

"Refine the idea of matter as much as you like; you will never transcend matter." (Z 753)

The otherworldly blue behind the head of Giovanni Bellini's *Doge Leonardo Loredan* at the National Gallery in London, offers a deliberately stark contrast to the face of the individual portrayed (as well as being opposite on the colour-circle to the flesh tones and bronze head band). One is taken by the contrast, necessarily, between the individual and the un-individuated sky of the background, if, indeed, it is sky. Italy does have such azure skies, so it is possible on some level to imagine the blue behind, or around the Doge's head to be a sky, but even so its flat contrast to his ornate garb and intricately depicted face could not be more striking. Standing in front of the painting one is initially drawn to the luminous brilliance of the face, the mesmerizingly exact detail of the aged man's eyes, his look out and past the viewer into some unseen realm. That look is at once stern and collected. He is removed from us, in a stiffly monumental pose, almost as if the painting depicts an utterly convincing waxwork. And yet, one is not free to abandon the face as mere facsimile so fresh and precise is its making. The face itself is uncanny, living and removed from life. On the verge of waking from a reverie, he looks past this world. Yet his vision is resolute.

This Renaissance portrait is one of the first to show a living subject face-on (usually reserved for gods and saints). If his ritual clothing seems to dominate any sense of a real body underneath that merely adds to the sense that here is a man inhabiting his role. The figure resembles a classical bust, suggesting a link to historical power and prestige. If the exact rendering and the impressive regalia announce a dominant physical presence, it is the blueness of the sky that provides the strongest alternative to the material world. With the boundary of the frame, and the tromp l'oeil frame and note ("Ioannes Bellinvs") placed beneath the image, we are shown the mundane world of the artist, our own world, the body; above this we have the lofty face of the sitter in all the pomp of Bellini's brilliant rendering; and finally surrounding all, or behind all, the blue, which is neither depiction, nor world, but a colour so vivid we must see it as hardly real but of the imagination.

We do see it of course, as a painting made 450 years ago, but we see also the liminal space between the rendering of the doge's vivid mortality and its halo of ideal blue. It is the contrast that marks the boundary between mortal and immortal, the edge between self and otherness. His eyes are themselves bluish, almost more a reflection of blue in his left eye, an idea of the sky in his very person. It is perhaps this thought that the eyes look out beyond the canvas towards, not a physical sight, but an idea somehow acknowledged in the perfection of blueness around him, an idea of his face against the face of the infinite. This is what all great portraits manage. In marking the individual perfectly, they point towards a universal mortality, and hence towards that which is not mortal. In great paintings materiality draws us towards the immaterial.

*

Leopardi's famous and beloved lyric *L'infinito* (Infinity) reflects something of the complexity of his ideas on Man's relationship to the extended world discovered and expressed in the writing of his masterpiece *Zibaldone* (Hotchpotch). As a 15 line lyric (deliberately outstripping the sonnet by one line? Pushing beyond its standard address?), it is a microcosm to the macrocosm of 1450 plus pages written over a 26 year period, which is itself a microcosm, as he intended it to be, of all Human ideas from the Ancient to the Modern (of which he must rank amongst the most immediate of heralds), written in Greek, Latin, French and occasionally English. Human ideas are themselves a small reckoning in the face of the Infinite.

Always dear to me this lonely hill
and hedge that hides the view
of the far horizon.
But sitting here and looking I can see

beyond, to endless space, superhuman emptiness
and deepest quiet that overwhelms
the heart until I almost faint. And when I hear the wind
that whispers through the trees
and then compare that silence
with this voice
the eternal comes to mind
and seasons gone and of the present
one alive and how it sounds,
Such that in this immensity my thought is drowned
And sweetly sinks into this endless sea.

Silence is a human dream. For mankind it is a form of listening. On the verge of silence the self awaits, ready for the next interruption. This interruption is the normal state of the human—a chattering sparrow—empty and promiscuous.

Begin reading *Infinity* and one notices the immediate placement of the physical site depicted, the hill, alongside the memory of the poet. This hill that the poem takes place upon, singled-out in deliberate deictic isolation, exists also as a declaration of memory for the poet. There is a need to notice that consciousness, memory and perception, act in tandem. There is no easy separation between the world and the thought of that world. The value of the hill is that it is small and knowable. The loneliness of the hill is, rather than pathetic fallacy, the human condition, a finite location in an unknown (and unknowable) universe. And as with the hilltop, this poem is an event of human experience, part memory, part perception, small, isolated, acknowledged against the vastness of the title.

The trajectory of the poem from sitting atop a small hill to drowning in a limitless sea, is equivalent, one might argue, to the biblical Flood. But Leopardi, a polemicist against Christianity and a materialist (probably an atheist), builds no ark. Instead, his pleasure is to drown in the limitless ocean of thought, a vast realm at once material and suggestive of the infinite.

For a subject (or an object) such as infinity the poem is deliberately slight, in size and detail. Leopardi emulates the fresh, limited strokes of Classical lyric poetry[1]—the poetry of "seasons gone." Classical authors "by just using a few strokes to describe and showing only a few parts of the object . . . allowed the imagination to wander among those vague and indeterminate ideas of childhood, which are born from ignorance of the whole." (Z 92) The brief details of the poem mimic the few graspable facts available to natural man, and recall the innocence and truthfulness of the classical imagination, which Leopardi felt had yet to move as far from Nature and real experience as the post-Roman imagination, stuffed as it is with rhetoric and propaganda (Leopardi felt Virgil's epics and Ovid's descriptive catalogues were overblown). In Leopardi's reckoning the development of the individual runs the same course as the history of culture[2]. The child is closer to culture's Classical beginnings, purer in ignorance, closer to the source of knowledge via the senses, rather than the obfuscating effects of learning. Leopardi's poem is from the perspective of a poet past childhood, knowledgeable enough to see the past as a now unattainable golden age, looking forward to oblivion.

The contemporary moment, the now of Modern culture, occupies the small hill of the present, with no clear vision of the future. But with that it is not hopeless. Leopardi's idyll offers a glimpse at least of resignation. The scene is personal and universal: "[a]nd a country scene for example, painted by the ancient poet with just a few strokes, without so to speak its horizon, would awaken in the imagination that divine surge of confused ideas, glowing with the indefinability of romance and the excess of precious, sweet strangeness and wonder, which was such ecstasy in our childhood." (Z 92) The ecstasy of childhood is partner to the fainting of the adult in line 7 (and the swooning of the last line). If this shuddering is reminiscent of the effects of the sublime, it is clearly not the Sublime of the Romantics,[3] produced by dramatic natural effects

---

1. "Leopardi preferred the 'grace' and 'simple' qualities of [Theocritus] to the 'sublime' Horace." (Galassi 420)

2. "In its poetic career, my spirit has followed the same course as the human spirit in general." (Z 116)

3. *Zibaldone* offers no rigorous reflections upon the sublime,

at work upon the senses. The scene is banal to such a degree that the senses are hardly engaged.

What the scene does allow is a sloughing off of the strictures of society: "In solitude, in the midst of delights of the countryside, man, being weary of the world, is able after a certain time to revert to a relationship with [Nature and inanimate things]. (Z 720) The scene is nested, the horizon is hidden and this allows for the birth of the infinite as the imagination wanders where the senses cannot:

> Sometimes the soul might desire, and actually does desire, a view that is restricted or confined in some way, as in Romantic situations. The reason is . . . a desire for the infinite, because then, instead of sight, the imagination is at work and the fantastic takes over from the real. The soul imagines what it cannot see, whether it is hidden by that tree, that hedge, that tower, and wanders in an imaginary space and pictures things in a way that would be impossible if its view could extend in all directions. (Z 132)

The soul then, what might that be? Though occasionally throughout *Zibaldone* he positions soul as counter to the body, this is often to work against traditional dualistic positions (in arguments against the immortality of the soul for example), and it is clear that Leopardi wishes us to see it as coterminous with matter: "It is regarded as paradoxical that matter can think. We set out convinced of its impossibility . . . that matter thinks is a fact. It is a fact because we ourselves think . . . It is a fact because we see that the modification of thoughts depend entirely upon sensations, upon our physical body. . . . It is a fact, because we feel our thought corporeally. (Z 1912-13)

---

mentioning it only in passing as an aesthetic category (referring briefly to Longinus) or merely as an adjective. In discussing "sublime sensations" caused by regarding the ancient, Leopardi suggests that the ancient produces "an indefinite sensation . . . an indeterminate time in which the soul loses itself." (Z 674) It seems that the sublime sensation is the swoon caused by imagining the infinite when unable to immediately discern boundaries. The sublime is the body's response to a rampant imagination.

The soul is an effect of thinking, an association of the mind[4], of consciousness, of the imagination, and as such connected directly to the senses, not a mysteriously immortal substance temporarily resident in the body. Its processes are of the body because "our mind is incapable not only of knowing but even of conceiving of anything beyond the bounds of matter. Beyond those bounds we cannot, try as we might, imagine a way of being, anything other than nothingness." (Z 316)[5] The soul cannot be outside of matter because matter is all that we are and the "[m]ind was not for Leopardi injected into matter from somewhere . . . humans are part of the flux of matter . . . [m]atter was itself intelligent, constantly mutating and producing new forms, some of them self-aware." (Gray 33-34). The soul is self-conscious matter.

Such materialism bears a strong resemblance to 20th century attempts to see the mind as a process of matter. In Lyotard's chapter "Matter and Time" from his wildly inclusive *The Inhuman*, matter is regarded as energy, and bodies are really only monadic instances of energy perceived from one point-of-view.[6] This point-of-view is provided by the mind which acts as

---

4. "Do we not observe the most diverse faculties in the soul? And among them memory, intellect, will, and imagination?" (Z 317)

5. And when we die, the soul dies, because as Diogenes puts it "being asked whether death is an evil thing, he replied, 'How can it be evil, when in its presence we are not aware of it?' " (Z 338) In breaking the self down to its constituent parts, Leopardi argues, "see if you can get to the atoms and particles that are indivisible and without parts. They will still be matter. Beyond them it is not spirit you will find but nothingness." (Z 753) And when the soul dies, "If we chose to regard the soul as material, this would immediately rule out the question of separation, and death would be nothing other than the extinction of the vital forces, which—whatever it consists of—is very rapidly extinguished." (Z 186)

6. Leopardi views matter as finite. Lyotard sees it as an infinite field of energy. Both agree, however, that the soul ought to be seen as a continuum of matter, and Lyotard's monadic model is not antithetical to Leopardi's idea of selfhood in this respect. Leopardi's disagreement with the Leibnizian monadic model was its employment of incorporeal being (see Z 732). Lyotard's materialist

a transformer, slowing energy exchanges (physical interactions of the body, perceptions) down sufficiently to suspend them in a realm of consciousness where the energy is self-regarding: "there are several families of transformers because there are several forms taken by energy: mechanical, calorific, electrical, rays, nuclear. Should we add thinking or spiritual energy, as Bergson used to put it?" (Lyotard 36). Yes, is his answer, "we must imagine that from matter to mind there is but a difference of degree, which depends on the capacity to gather and conserve. Mind is matter which remembers its interactions, its immanence. But there is a continuum from the instantaneous mind of matter to the very gathered matter of mind." (Lyotard 40). So, the human is a transformer, in particular the human is marked by the transformative capacity of the mind: "The further one climbs the ladder of organized beings, the more one observes that the immediate reaction is delayed." (Lyotard 41) The characteristic delay for humanity is thinking (with the concomitant faculty of memory), the results of which lead to "indeterminacy, unpredictability and growing freedom of the actions these beings can perform." (Lyotard 41) Even so, "the transformer that is our central nervous system . . . can only transcribe and inscribe according to its own rhythm the excitations which come to it from the milieu in which it lives." (Lyotard 43). His use of tran*scribe* and in*scribe* highlights the elaborate involvement of language and the written in the development of our transformer. Language is an effective capacitor[7]. The mind thinks with language, as Leopardi puts it "each

version replaces God's management of the universe with energy, and identifies energy with matter, doing away with the duality Leopardi rejected in Leibniz.

7. Poems offer an off-site performance of the process of thinking, slowing the display of events of individuality down to such a degree they appear to be outside of time altogether (because they are outside of the corruptible body of the poet). But they are themselves another multi-layered apparatus that exchanges energy (needing physical as well as psychical energy to be written and read), offering themselves as intricate and uncanny models of the self-conscious events of being.

person thinks in . . . the language that is most familiar to him (Z 455).

Prior to the transformations of consciousness there is the nothingness of non-being—an unmediated array of energy exchanges unmonitored by a point-of-view. Consciousness provides an arena whereby some of the small events of our perception are acknowledged—but for Leopardi and for many subsequent thinkers it is also where the instigation of selfhood is drawn into isolation against an apparently infinite otherness that the self can only ever not be[8].

Throughout *Zilbadone* Leopardi revisits the concept of the infinite. His initial thoughts suggest that the infinite might be identified with nothingness: "[Infinity] does not exist neither can it exist except in the imagination or in language, but which is a quality proper to and inseparable from the idea and from the word nothingness, which itself does not exist except in thought or in language, and as it is thought of or expressed in language." (Z 1827) There is nowhere for the human to encounter the infinite, or nothingness except as a linguistic idea. It is the imagination that allows for the prospect of the immaterial, even as the imagination remains rooted to the material self: "Nothing in Nature actually announces infinity, the existence of anything infinite. Infinity is a production of our imagination, and at the same time our smallness... [what] we cannot conceive of, we have thought of as infinite." (Z 1824) Infinity is the imagination's way of dealing with plenitude. This can happen with sight: "The belief that the universe is infinite is an optical illusion, that at least is my view . . . I believe . . . it most probable that the infinity of the universe is only a natural illusion of the imagination". (Z 1915) That we know that the world exists beyond that which we can see allows the imagination to conceive of matter extending infinitely. But Leopardi also con-

---

8. This dominant figure of an isolated self is of course only one metaphorical way of understanding the phenomenon of being (if by far the most prevalent—so as to seem almost inevitable). The isolated self might instead be seen as occurrences of self-conscious energy exchanges without worrying about isolation. Indeed this seems to be one obvious outcome of defining soul as matter.

nects our concept of infinity to our natural insatiable desire.
He believes desire, and the quest for pleasure is a fundamental
and natural human activity. Individual needs can be fulfilled,
but desire itself doesn't end, it shifts to find new needs. This
endless process of searching can be seen as transcending the
material, in that the material never satisfies the quest, but "[t]
he sense of the nothingness of all things . . . and our tendency towards an infinite . . . comes perhaps from a very simple
cause . . . one that is more material than spiritual. The human
soul always essentially desires . . . this desire and this tendency has no limits, because it is inborn or born along with existence itself . . . such a nature carries infinity materially within
it, for every single pleasure is circumscribed, but not pleasure
itself." (Z 129) The infinite nature of desire is really the imagination supplying the metaphor of an unbounded realm within which the concept of desire, as opposed to finite instances
of desiring, might exist. It is the imagination trying to understand generalities of human nature beyond its own specific experience. But such a realm is only brought to mind in relation
to the notion of the plenitude of matter. And we can see such a
concept only from the position of our own selfhood: "We ourselves are unable to discourse on the nature of those beings of
which we cannot conceive . . . a being placed outside of matter." (Z 318) The imaginative faculty in man is such that it can
itself "conceive of things that do not exist . . . the infinite pleasure that cannot be found in reality can thus be found in the
imagination . . . human happiness cannot consist in anything
other than imagination and illusion,"(Z 130) illusion in the
form of myth and religious faith, imagination in the play of
poetry and art.

   As the poem moves past the initial point-of-view of
the hill, we encounter the imagination taking over from the
limited perspective of the senses. Instead of images of a poetic countryside idyll, we are confronted with "endless space, superhuman emptiness/and deepest quiet," the nothingness that
Leopardi positions as the limit of our experience as 'thinking
matter,' the 'infinite nothing' that is beyond our condition of
being. There are no descriptions, just a run of abstract super-

latives and negatives, nothing we encounter other than as an idea. At this juncture the poet's experience is at its farthest remove from the presence of his material being in the world (or his being material in the world) and from his descriptive abilities. The poem is forced to the end of its resourcefulness. Such feelings of the infinite, and it is a feeling of the idea that Leopardi recounts, take place at the end of meaning:

> At the height of passion's fervor a poet is a poet no more; he can't write poetry at this moment. In the presence of nature, his whole soul is taken up with the image of the infinite, ideas thronging his mind, he is incapable of distinguishing, choosing, or grasping any of them . . . you can't express the infinite when you are feeling it, only afterward: and when the finest poets wrote lines that roused our sense of wonder for the infinite, their minds were not filled with any sensation of the infinite; conjuring up the infinite, they weren't feeling it. (Parks 52–53)

The fear of the loss of self, the self on the cusp of otherness, is felt in the body (where else?), where the experience of the idea of the infinite, is enough to overwhelm the heart ("*Il cor non si spaura*"), as one might expect when confronted with one's own non-being. The sensation of this fear, a swoon or faint, calls the mind back to the body from its furthest horizon of abstractions.

It is the human-scaled voice of the wind in the trees that calls the poet back to his senses. The poem (and the self) has survived the vertiginous extensions of the imagination, which will now enter the faculty of memory. The voice in the trees, the music of the actual world, is companionable to the poet's voice writing his simple song. The flight of his imagination threatened the event of language, only to be brought back by the panicked heart and engaged by the song in the trees. The poem houses both the idea of the infinite, albeit it an abstraction, and the finite experience manifest through the senses. These two are held as extremes (the extremes that are often separated into mind and body), but they are presented as parts of a continuum. It is the swing between these polarities of material existence, the physical and the spiritual, that provide the boundaries of human experience; one facing nature with the senses, the other facing the divine with the imagination (grappling with the concept of the infinite). And it is the pleasure of swoon[9] of the exultant imagination that gives the sweet to the contemplative's sense of drowning in a vast ocean. The ocean is that vast otherness unknown to our being [10], as well as the capacity of our own finite soul to house the idea of the unfathomable infinite at the furthest reaches of its knowing. The sweet knowledge of the poem is the boundary of self sunk in a sea of ignorance.

*

The blue otherness of sky looks from a distance like it must have been painted in one stroke (any artist today attempting such a pure coat of utter blue would have to use an air-brush), but on closer inspection one can make out the tiniest of inconsistencies of colour, minute brushstrokes of darker blue amidst the flat lighter blue, that then draw attention to the texture of myriad brushstrokes making up the entire blue field. To the viewer's right, abutting the shadowed neck and hat of the Doge, the blue becomes hazier, almost losing colour, as if part of the shadow from the hat and neck is reflecting in the sky itself. One can see that the tiny brush has been held perpendicularly to the curve of the outline and brushed away from the figure outwards into the field. I'd guess that the blue was painted after the figure, and that the defining junction of figure and background was finalized with the addition of the blue. Here then, we have the otherness of the sky, the background, as the necessary other that defines the isolated self. It's implication of an infinite otherness is made with the subtlest of fine strokes, small dabs of colour that beggar belief, but are, in fact, finite

---

9. See footnote 2 in this chapter.

10. One is reminded of Nabokov's famous opening to his auto biography, *Speak Memory*, where he describes his birth: "The cradle rocks above an abyss, and common sense tells us that our existence is but a brief crack of light between two eternities of darkness."

in number, made of the self-same substance as the face, by the same hand. The divine is made by the mundane, the work of the body pushed to the edge of the possible. The idea of the infinite is housed in a finite body.

Works Cited

Gray, John, *The Soul of the Marionette.* New York: Farrar, Straus and Giroux, 2015.

Leopardi, Giacomo. *Canti.* Translated by Jonathan Galassi. London: Penguin, 2010.

—. *Passions.* Translated by Tim Parks. New Haven: Yale University Press, 2014.

—. *Zibaldone.* Edited by Michael Caesar and Franco D'Intino. New York: Farrar, Straus and Giroux, 2013.

Lyotard, Jean-Francois. *The Inhuman.* Translated by Geoffrey Bennington and Rachel Bowby. Stanford: Stanford University Press, 1991.

2 The Poet's Tomb

for Alice and her chorus of Ghouls.

I. When *Me fecit* Becomes *Hic Jacet*

Legend had it that Virgil[1] wrote his own epitaph. A legend of a legend of a legend if you like.

> *Mantua me genuit, Calabri rapuere, tenet nunc*
> *Parthenope. Cecini pascua, rura, duces.*

(Mantova gave me life, Calabria stole me away, Naples holds me now; I sang of pastures, farms, commanders.)

It succinctly maps a geographical history from his place of birth, to the translation of his body, and subsequent burial, balanced by a following list of his literary output: The Eclogues (pastures), The Georgics (farms) and his most ambitious work The Aeneid (the history of Aeneas and the founding of Rome). The form encourages us to link the three place names into an irresistible relation with each of his three works.

His birthplace of Mantua links easily enough to ideas of a happy pastoral youth, a golden age. It might have been Virgil's wish to be buried in his beloved Naples, it was apparently also his wish that his unfinished masterpiece, The Aeneid be burned. Saved from the pyre, the work survived the burial of the poet and carried the name of Virgil to future genera-

---

1. Even Virgil's name is the stuff of legend. Publius Vergilius Maro. Publius was a common enough praenomen, though it is interesting that for one so shy destined to be so famous, it means public. His cognomen, Maro is anagrammatic of both *Amor* and *Roma*, the subjects of his Aeneid. Some speculate the etymological root of the name Virgil is *vigil*, a time of purposeful wakefulness easily imagined for the poet at his craft; others *virga*, or wand, suggesting that his poetic gifts verged on the magical. It is recorded that the day before his birth his mother dreamt of giving birth to a laurel branch, that once planted immediately bloomed and bore fruit, portentous of his poetic career.

tions. In that sense we might see his great work as the final resting place of his name. It's harder to draw an easy parallel between *"Calabri rapuere"* and the work of the Georgics, seven years in the making.

A recent New York Times article translates the epitaph as ''Mantua was my birthplace; I died in Calabria; and now I rest at Parthenope. I sang of pastures, farms and leaders.''[2] Live, die, buried has a nice balance, but *rapuere* does not mean die. Bernard Knox prefers "Mantova gave me life, The Calabrians took it away . . . "[3] Better is Kimberly Johnson's version with "Mantua bore me, Calabria seized me, now Naples holds me."[4]

Virgil died in Brundisium, (Brindisi) in Apulia bordering Calabria, so it seems that the reference to the Calabrian *rape*[5], might be the temporary and unlawful theft of his body, awaiting his fitting burial near Naples. It's possible and popular to read the "abduction" of *rapuere* as a metaphorical reference to death, but the nefarious act of *rape* or abduction, sounds very much like a Neopolitan slur,[6] at least an affirmation that his body is now home where it belongs. Death, a theft, is merely second in the epitaph's movement, from birth the poet was stolen from us, temporarily. Death's just the translation from

2. "Who is buried in Virgil's Tomb?" by James Shapiro, NYT, March 21st, 1999. http://www.nytimes.com/1999/03/21/books/who-is-buried-in-virgil-s-tomb.html?pagewanted=all

3. Virgil *The Aeneid* trans. Robert Fagles (Penguin Classics, New York, 2006), 11

4. Virgil *The Georgics: A Poem of the Land*, ed. Kimberly Johnson (New York: Penguin, 2009).

5. *Medieval Texts in Translation*, eds Katherine l. Jansen, Joanna Drell & Frances Andrews (UPenn Press, 2010): "Virgil, who was of the Lombard race . . . died in the 25th year of Octavian's rule in the city of Brindisi, whence his body was later stolen by the Calabrians and brought to Naples," 524.

6. The Calabrians would have been considered rough and criminal by the Neopolitans. He died of a fever that he caught in Megara, so yes, his life was snatched from him at 50, it seems unfair that the Calabrians themselves (or Calabria) be held accountable!

his mortal birth to his poetical immortality, "here" marked by a stone. The grave replaces the poet's body (his birth) via the transaction of his death. It becomes the final resting place for his writing, mirroring the translation from the body to the poem, the act of writing. In the logic of the epitaph the scheme seems to form an equivalence between Poet-poem-reader and birth-death(abduction)-burial(immortality). It is as if the central act of the poet's life, his poetry, is directly linked to death or abduction. More than life-affirming, poems seem to be deaths in search of a resting place?

The rhetorical balance of the epitaph also links death or abduction with his middle work, and there is of course one famous abduction that *The Georgics* does deal with, that of Eurydice to the Underworld. The fourth book deals ostensibly with beekeeping, but towards the end of the chapter the story shifts from bees, to look at the miracle of life and death, and in particular the tale of Orpheus.

The shepherd Aristaeus, thrown into despair at the loss of his bees to sickness, bemoans his fate to his mother Cyrene, the water nymph. His lament proves potent and he is invited into the nymphs' own realm where he is advised to capture the shape-shifting seer Proteus. Proteus reveals that the gods are angry with the shepherd for chasing Eurydice to her untimely death. Here we are treated to a description of Orpheus, singing in sad solitude a song that penetrates even to the depths of Dis, where the poet enters the gates of Taenarum. All of Hades is spellbound by his song, even Cerberus slack-jawed, and Ixion's wheel halted. Returning ahead of his lover, bound by a fatal oath, on the very verge of light, he turns and in that act, forgetting himself, all is lost, she returns again to smoke while "he vainly clutched at the shadows with so much left unsaid."[7] It is no coincidence then that she vanishes and he loses the ability to find his words, for really what has occurred is the end of his song. Her name in his verse promises her life. It is the poem's task to bridge that verge, that penumbra is shadow between the eternal realm of the poem's voice and the living

7. Virgil, *Eclogues, Georgics, Aeneid 1-6* trans. H.R. Fairclough (Loeb Classical Library, Cambridge, 1999). 255

poet (or the living reader) returning to the world of flesh from his lament. The spell of Orpheus's verse ends in a catastrophe of the self-conscious ending (verse from verso, closed by his body's famous turn), or with unself-conscious inarticulation. Without words to recall his ghost he is left with nothing, the image fades, like the Keatsian speaker in *the Nightingale*, waking out of the dream of the poem, dying.

Seven months of wandering laments ends with the Ciconian women, the maenads (apparently resenting his devotion), tearing the poet limb from limb, his head thrown into the Hebrus where it floats still singing "Ah, poor Eurydice." The book ends with Aristaeus's successful sacrifice of four bullocks and a goat, whose corpses miraculously fill with swarms of new bees. His price to the gods has been paid. Orpheus's fate is to exist in a song endlessly inhabiting a lament, a kind of purgatorial realm. Such, perhaps, is the fate of those who give their names to poems. Their death is held off by the recitation of their words, each reading of their work rekindling their voice in lament, echoing (mirroring) the task of Orpheus bringing his dead lover back to life (as long as his song is sustained). The poem presents itself as a habitat for the ever-absent lover, disinterring even as there is no body and no ground. Orpheus the poet does not find his own grave. It makes sense that we build our poets tombs. They are the surrogate physical sites of an ever-absent body.

*

The Greek word *sema* means both *sign* and *grave*. "For the Greeks," according to Robert Pogue Harrison[8], "the grave marker was not just one sign among others. It was a sign that signified the source of signification itself, since it 'stood for' what it 'stood in'—the ground of burial as such." The grave was the coincidence of sign and ground, the grounding of language as such, and therefore the place par excellence of human foundation. It is signification of death that presents the encoun-

---

8. Harrison, Robert Pogue *The Dominion of the Dead* (Chicago: University of Chicago Press, 2003), 21.

ter between the place where we disappear and the place we are able to signify (evidence of our presence). The *hic* of *hic jacet* is "no ordinary locative adverb. Like the ancient *sema*, it is an indicator that appropriates the ground of indication."⁹ We know that with the marking of *hic jacet*, here lies, we are pointing to an absence. But we have given ourselves the gift of somewhere to point.

In his *wunderkammer, The Origin of Consciousness in the Breakdown of the Bicameral Mind*, Julian Jaynes proposes, amongst a myriad other brilliant propositions, that the gathering of civilization, the shift from hunter gatherer groups of 20 or 30 primitives, to the "civilized" township of 200 or more takes place because of two interrelated events: the invention of names and the subsequent invention of graves: "when a person dies, the name still goes on, and hence burial practices and mourning."¹⁰ But another important thing happens with the development of names. Previous to this, there was no "source" for speech (Jaynes supports a theory of speech as a kind of hallucination, an unprecedented happening). Once names are recognized, speech develops as a social interaction, Gods and rulers become possible, and poets. What is most controversial and intriguing about Jaynes's theory is the idea that language precedes self-consciousness. Humans had the ability to speak before they settled on the idea that it was a "self" speaking. Rather than language being a projection of a self, language becomes the arena where the idea of selfhood can develop: "before an individual . . . had an interior self, he unconsciously first posited it in others . . . we may first unconsciously suppose other consciousnesses, and then infer our own by generalization!"¹¹ Language and even our names come to us from the outside. What might seem stranger to most of us is that even consciousness does: we "locate this space of consciousness inside our own heads . . . [but] we know perfectly well that there is no such

9. Ibid., 22.

10. Jaynes, Julian *The Origin of Consciousness in the Breakdown of the Bicameral Mind* (Boston: Mariner Books, 2000), 136

11. Ibid., 217. Compare to Lacan's mirror stage.

space in anyone's heads at all!"[12] Indeed "in reality, consciousness has no location whatever except as we imagine it has."[13] And of course we continue to imagine. Cultures and religions have been based on the quest for this absent place.

This absence is constitutional to language and being. Language provides the medium within which the human can contemplate their own absence, their mortality, and poems (laments in particular) thematize this in a self-conscious enactment.

The mystery of the epitaph contains within it a mystery that all tombs display: what of the dead lies here at all[14]? Like a poem, the tomb's foundation is the name of the absent person it proposes housing. If we supposed Virgil to have authored his own epitaph, we also know that he cannot be witness to his own burial; he cannot be the authority of his own internment[15].

Of course the identity of any speaker is not the physical person of the poet. In order to use language we enter into communal signification. What the poem and the grave share is not the person of the poet, but the signification of the absent author.[16]

---

12. Ibid., 45

13. Ibid., 46

14. The epitaph, and most of what we know about Virgil, comes down to us through Donatas's fourth-century version of a lost second-century biography by Suetonius. It offers scant information riddled with subsequent rumours about a man famed for his shyness.

15. The legend that he was the author mimics his own literary exploits. The gesture of the legend is really only what all acts of language perform. In witnessing his own death he becomes a worker of miracles. He was ripe for canonization, his supposed tomb turned into a shrine. In the middle ages his legend grew to include acts of magic beyond mere mortals. By visiting his tomb, Dante and Petrarch (and much later Leopardi), were seeking to draw favourable connections from physical proximity to his final resting place. Their act was a physical correlative to the act of reading his poetry.

16. It is this same common medium however that provides us with the apparatus of our memory, that we will use to recall being, constructing and identifying ourselves as an individual as such.

In taking the first person of the epitaph literally, we see the folding of mortality into the immortal seeming nature of language, and the desire for the poet to overcome the boundaries of life and death in the immortality of his or her own work. Orpheus or Virgil, in choosing to visit the underworld in their art touched on the privilege of the gods. The poem hangs between both worlds, the physical and the immortal. So when we read of Orpheus bringing to life that which was inanimate, it is merely the mirror to using immortal (seeming) language to signify the living. The miracle of the poem is to cross the border between realms. It is a small step to animate the dead other. It is merely the shadow's other side. The poem is the middle act between the living and the dead. It is the translation or *rapuere*[17].

So to Virgil's masterpiece: *The Aeneid*. Here his reputation rests. Here his immortality resides. We might say such things, but what do they really mean? Here in Book VI we see Aeneas's descent to the underworld. His journey relies more on his heritage than any skill as a poet. When the Cumaean Sybil replies to his request to see his father, it is with his heritage fore-fronted "Born of the blood of gods, Anchises' son, man of Troy, the descent to the underworld is easy."[18] During the funeral of Misenus (the rightful end of life), he is led away by his mother's doves to the Golden Bough, his gift for Proserpina, assuring safe passage via the dark lake Avernus to the underworld. Before making it to the Elysium fields, Aeneas encounters a catalogue of the damned and unburied. Some of these are worthies such as Palinurus who seeks proper burial, for as Charon informs us "Not until bones have found a last Resting place will shades be let across these gurgling currents."[19] So it is that our mortal life is a passage from birth to

17. The Calabrian abduction seems to parallel the act of writing itself, as a body carried across the stygian gap between the living and the dead. In a sense every poem is an epitaph, accompanied by the common wish for the poet's voice to sound beyond the grave.

18. Virgil *The Aeneid* trans. Robert Fagles (New York: Penguin, 2006), 186.

19. Heaney, Seamus *Aeneid Book VI* (New York: Farrar, Straus and Giroux, 2016), 35.

burial. Without the rites of burial and the building of a shrine, our journey remains unfinished. Anchises shares a march of future Roman heroes with Aeneas, securing Rome as a resting site for Trojan victory. It might be said that the whole purpose of the Aeneid is to secure for Rome a viable Trojan Heritage, secure for Rome an ancestry. The Aeneid is Rome's Odyssey and Iliad. It's the Hebrew Bible in terms of tribal history securing a link between the actions of gods and the clan. Civilizations are literally and historically based upon the graves of their ancestors. And their epics.

If Rome's soul is housed in Virgil's masterpiece, it's funny to think that Naples, not Rome, houses his monument. But perhaps it was Virgil's wish to be seen as an Aeneas, ancestor to an Empire, alighting near Naples to secure his legacy.

In his perambulating classic "Poets in a Landscape" Gilbert Highet describes his journey to Virgil's tomb:

> Entering the park, we step out of the present into an enclave of the past . . . Approaching the rocky face, we see a huge cave receding into black darkness. It might almost be the grotto of the Sibyl at Cumae, where Aeneas learned how to enter the underworld . . . the wall bears...a copy of the epitaph of Vergil . . . On a crag above the park . . . stands a Roman tomb, small, unassuming, anonymous . . . On its wall, a scholarly visitor of the Renaissance carved a latin inscription, which expresses both our disappointment at the absence of any true relic of Vergil, and of our sense that here his memory still lingers:
>
> Ravaged the tomb, and broken the urn. Nothing remains.
>
> And yet the poet's name exalts the place.[20]

Nothing is left but the rumor of Virgil's tomb. Stories begin with his request to be buried somewhere between Naples and Pozzuoli, near a small farm left to him by his teacher Siron.

20. Highet, Gilbert. "Poets in a Landscape." *New York Review of Books* (2010), 81-82.

A century later we have records of Statius visiting the site and composing beneath the tomb, and Silius Italicus (author of the longest Latin poem written) purchased both Virgil's and Cicero's graves, hoping perhaps to be remembered by that proximity at least. The great Bay tree planted there was said to have died along with Dante. Petrarch visited. Boccaccio dedicated his life to writing there, "But apparently, during the Dark ages, the exact situation of the burial-place was forgotten; the tomb itself was probably destroyed during the barbarian wars."[21] Some say that in 1326 Robert of Anjou removed the urn to the Castel Nuevo for safekeeping, others that it was given by the Government to a cardinal from Mantua, who died at Genoa on his way home. What remains are signs replacing signs, trees replacing trees, shades and stories. Naturally enough every dark recess is empty.

This empty tomb leads us from the Pagan epic, to the Christian era.

II. Keats and Shelley and Their Watery Grave.

Keats wrote his own epitaph as well. Sort of.

> This grave contains all that was Mortal of a Young English Poet Who on his Death Bed, in the Bitterness of his Heart at the Malicious Power of his Enemies Desired these Words to be engraven on his Tomb Stone: *Here lies One Whose Name was writ in Water. 24 February 1821.*

Surrounded as if by the handiwork of the anonymous engraver, the bitter framework almost overwhelms the apparent simplicity of Keats's final message. In *Adonais*, his elegy-homage to Keats, Shelley (along with seeming to predict his own death by drowning) sides with the tone of Keats's memorial in holding Keats's critics part way responsible for exacerbating the consumption that carried him off, in his little bedroom staring up at the blue painted ceiling, listening to the gurgling *Barcaccia* in the *Piazza di Spagna* (boat-shaped to commemorate the site where one washed up at the height of the 1598 flood).

---

21. Ibid., 79.

Keats's epitaph has a number of literary precedents. Catullus's bitter epigram (LXX) on his lover's intention to marry him is perhaps the first instant:

> My lover says that she'd prefer to marry no one
>> But me, even if Jupiter asked for her love
> Ah yes: but what a woman says to an eager lover
>> Write it on running water, write it on air[22]

This might be relevant for a poet who never fulfilled his obvious desire to marry Fanny, but for an epitaph the most obvious echo is of Beaumont and Fletcher's play *Philaster* (Act V, Scene III), in which Philaster rebukes the King for his threat against his beloved Arethusa:

Sir, let me speak next;
And let my dying words be better with you   84
Than my dull living actions. If you aim
At the dear life of this sweet innocent,
You are a tyrant and a savage monster,
That feeds upon the blood you gave a life to;   88
Your memory shall be as foul behind you,
As you are living; all your better deeds
Shall be in water writ, but this in marble;
No chronicle shall speak you, though your own,   92
But for the shame of men. No monument,
Though high and big as Pelion, shall be able
To cover this base murder: make it rich
With brass, with purest gold and shining jasper,   96
Like the Pyramides; lay on epitaphs
Such as make great men gods; my little marble
That only clothes my ashes, not my faults,
Shall far outshine it.

Philaster cannot threaten the life of his Monarch, but he can target that part of the King that is immortal, his reputation.

---

22. Highet, 32

His few good deeds will be illegible, *writ in water,* an imperma-
nence contrasting the longer lasting nature of a marble record of
his bad name, the fitting epitaph or burial.

If *writ in water* describes Keats's literary reputation, it
seems coy given that he felt somewhat secure about the future of
his own poetry[23]. What seems more in question, and more com-
plicated is just what of himself that reputation, that name, or
even his own work contained. We see Keats grappling with death
throughout his writing, pressing upon the inscrutable link between living and writing and writing and dying.

In *I stood tip-toe upon a hill*[24] *(1816),* Keats invites his reader to "[l[inger a while upon some bending planks", the presence
of the body registered only in the negative as a bend in the plank.
Here the self becomes viewer and participant as much as bodied
individual:

And watch intently Nature's gentle doings . . .
How silent comes the water round that bend;
Not the minutest whisper does it send . . .
Why you might read two sonnets, ere they [floating grass] reach
To where the hurrying freshnesses aye preach
A natural sermon o'er their pebbly bed. (lines 63-71)

And the passive poet, present only as a viewer (or a reader of
sonnets), is there to hear the water perform her own sermon.
The performance, we imagine, is specific to the occasion and
the audience. The sermon is a pantheistic song witnessed in the
instant. Water has always been the haunt of muses, the babble
suggestive of rhythm and language for the poet to take up, be
taken up by.[25] What it sings is relation. The water is silent until

---

23. Letter to George Oct 25th, 1818 "I think I shall be among the English
Poets after my death."

24. Keats, John *Selected Poems* ed. John Barnard (New York: Penguin,
2007), 13.

25. "Let this fair laurel grow on the fresh bank,/and he who planted it,
in its sweet shade,/to watery sounds, write high and happy thoughts."
Petrarch, Selections from the Canzoniere, trans. Mark Musa (New York:
Oxford World Classics, 2008), 53

it encounters the otherness of the pebbles. Silent also until the poet listens. Song is the resonance of natural encounters, it is not an act in isolation, but a conversation. As soft and fleeting as this babble might be, we see the human ear counts it into poetic form, two sonnets worth. The poet and the babbling water, object and subject, mirror each other with their share of authority and passivity. Herein is life, self in relation. But herein also is death:

> From the quaint mossiness of agèd roots:
> Round which is heard the spring-head of clear waters
> babbling so wildly of its lovely daughters
> the spreading blue-bells—it may haply mourn
> that such fair clusters should be rudely torn
> from their fresh beds, and scattered thoughtlessly
> by infant hands, left on the path to die. (lines 40-46)

The passage contrasts young with old, the fresh clear water singing as it rounds the old mossy roots. Even more strikingly the flowers (poesies=poetries) are plucked from life by infant hands. This human intrusion is clearly a projection of Keats's own awareness of the life/death cycle. Water here is symbolic of life, feeding its daughters, the blue-bells (the water nymph/muses) as it sings. Its song is unself-conscious, merely reactive until the human consciousness enters in the form of the infant (a surrogate for Keats). The river has no sentimental concerns for the flowers until they are plucked. The thoughtless scattering suggests that the child is not yet fully conscious of the full meaning of the death of the flowers, but the poem knows.

It is the inclusion of the child's hand that brings in an acknowledgement of death, though it may be hinted at with the old mossy root. The flowers are so beautiful she wants to take them up somehow, acknowledge their vivacity, but plucking them serves only to disappoint (Keats is forever famously reaching his hands towards that which he cannot grasp[26]). We cannot hold life, so the poesy is "left on the path to die." Were

---

26. "This living hand now warm and capable," *Selected Poems*, 237

he a babbling brook he would not draw up the flowers hopefully to preserve them. As a poet, his human consciousness is
doomed to notice the thrum of life and to want to take hold of
it, co-opt it for himself:

> Where swarms of minnows show their little heads
> Staying their waxy bodies against the streams,
> To taste the luxury of sunny beams . . .
> If you but scantily hold out a hand
> That very instant not one will remain
> But turn your eye, and they are there again. (lines 72-80)

Here Keats self-consciously interrupts the balance of
immediate interplay by trying to take hold of a single minnow
(which is a reflection of his own subjectivity). It isn't until
he turns away that the scene becomes whole again. His on-
looking self-conscious nature is the only thing allowing him
to notice the events and it's the very thing stopping him from
entering in.

   The babbling river song is the sound excess of the
actions of its interactive course. In the human world poetry
marks the evidence of interaction between the self and other. But just like the child with the blue-bells, we cannot pluck
the living and preserve it in a poem. Only by interactions can a
poem happen, but much like the hand of Midas, anything the
poem touches turns to words.

   In his famous *The Nightingale (1819)*[27], Keats worries on
the poem as a fleeting place of interaction. Right at the close of
the poem, the speaker (designated as the self-conscious nature
of the author) "notices" the approaching end of the poem, and
follows the fate of the author returning to the living world. The
spell, the magical interlude of the poem, must end, and the author must return to other actions and interactions. The speaker then, must "die," the poetic voice now silent, left to haunt
the vales of the poem, but it is the speaker or the living poet
who feels bereft?

---

27. Ibid., 193

Forlorn! The very word is like a bell
to toll me back me back to my sole self . . .
fled is that music—Do I wake or sleep? (lines 71-80)

The tolling bell is a funereal ending to the poem wherein Keats once again self-consciously examines the gesture the poem makes as he's making it/it's making him. The drama of this ending is to question what of the self exists in the poem, and if it remains there, what of the self returns to the real world.

In *I stood tip-toe*, Keats has already seen how singing is the excess of (selves in) interaction, and that nothing, no "self" exists (or sings) in isolation. For Keats his own poems offer a realm where he might encounter "otherness" as he follows (and aims) the imagined bird off beyond the senses of his body "on the viewless wings of poesy". For Keats the issue at hand is working out which of these "others" is himself? The speaker is no more Keats than the bird is.

Or, the poem is the only place the poet engages in the wild abandon of excess we find in the babbling stream, to fall silent again until the next excess of expression. A poet is not only a human person walking the world, but one with the facility to dissolve into a realm of wordy exchange where subjectivity and objecthood vie and shift[28]. The human that wakes out of *The Nightingale*, comes back merely to mortality and to other interactions, holding the remnants of the trance. The poem falls into its silent latency, awaiting a reader's future, a plucked flower, laid down in the road for future walkers to notice. As much as he loves the beauty of the thrum of life, his is the clumsy infant hand grasping at life, ripping it up by the roots, and once more holding the dying thing. That's why the bell of "forlorn" rings.

A poem is a self-conscious artifact, a memorial to the ephemeral. It is artifice, poignant and confounding, vital to a self that notices the passing world. The dream of some eternal realm haunts Keats's poetry, just as the knowledge that that

---

28. Consonant with Keats's concept of *Negative Capability*, where the poet becomes universally receptive, rather than assertive and controlling.

realm is beyond his mortal claim. Self-consciousness shows us ourselves looking at the world, gives us knowledge of our life at the same instant that it shows us death. Nature's song is a flower in all its glory, but the poem holds the flower apart, leaves the dead flower in the road for the next traveller. Keats notices the babbling stream from his bridge, but he is not in the stream.

What this really describes is the negative place of language as the absent ground of self-consciousness. Hegel, a near contemporary of Keats looked to this negativity in his *Phenomenology of Spirit* (1807). He starts with the concept of *sense-certainty*, a sensual impression of an object in the world, which seems our most immediate way of grasping reality, but demonstrates that we can only take hold of this sense-certainty via the abstraction of language. When we look at the act of seeing the object, we see two aspects of being, the "I" and the "this" of the object, exist simultaneously in necessary separation. Thus "within sense-certainty itself"[29] we find that the "object . . . is posited as what is unessential and mediated, something which is sense-certainty is not *in itself* but through [the mediation of] an other, the "I."[30] The "immediate being" is then a form of mediation, as the known object requires the knowing other. When we speak of the object we might say "'this' bit of paper on which I am writing . . . but what [we] mean is not what [we] say. If [we] actually wanted to say 'this' bit of paper which [we] mean, if [we] wanted to *say* it, then this is impossible, because the sensuous This cannot be reached by language, which belongs to consciousness.[31] But the "I" doesn't become the placeholder for this knowing either. "Sense-certainty . . . comes to know that its essence is neither in the object nor in the "I."[32] For when I speak of an "I" it is "merely universal like 'Now', "Here', or "This' in general."[33] Language is the realm of me-

29. Hegel, G.W.F. *Hegel's Phenomenolgy of Spirit*, trans. A.V.Miller (Oxford: Oxford University Press, 1977), 59.

30. Ibid., 59

31. Ibid., 66

32. Ibid ., 66

33. Ibid., 62

diation, the place of consciousness, a place between self and other. Instead of marking a specific place Language marks the event of the perception. Rather than presenting the immediate object "and instead of knowing something immediate I take the truth of it, or perceive it."[34] In the conscious event of noticing an object we have replaced the certainty of the sensed object with the truth of perception. The truth we garner is the universal event of language. This is a negative realm in that every element is constituted upon otherness, and within language we can neither reach the object it describes nor the self doing the describing. Rather than linking a trace back to the earth or the body, language presents these elements negatively making that link impossible.

How do we then return to the immediate world in full consciousness? We do not. And this is the dilemma that Keats pushes on in much of his poetry. That element that seems constitutional to being, our consciousness, is a universal otherness, apart from the body and the world. We cannot reach into the world with a poem. We are stuck on the bridge.

So where does this leave his epitaph? If the water is immediate physicality, a kind of unself-conscious song of the world, then writing in it is always impossible, always somewhere else. As a physical act, writing on water performs the impossibility of the two realms co-existing. The flower in the world is immediately a part of the world until it is seen by a consciousness as an object. Writing it down is like plucking the flower. And all we have of Keats in the poem is the absent child that left the flower in the road. His poems know this. They are often about it. And so is his epitaph.

A name writ in water is a failed epitaph, impermanent, ridiculous. The idea that his "name was writ" might suggest that others (critics) had writ his name in water to throw away his legacy, but the idea that Keats can write his own epitaph shows him somehow claiming a more universal frailty of being: the life of the body and the life of consciousness offer us two separate elements; the body dies every time a word is spoken, it dies into articulation, lifted from immediacy into oth-

---

34. Ibid., 62

erness. Each word is an epitaph of sorts. In language the poet has already died. Is he mourning the fact that nothing of the body can be saved? Well it seems to be both yes and no. Keats seems to know something of Hegel's reasoning, but rather than be consoled by philosophic truths, he responds with sadness.

For Keats, the view from the bridge is intoxicating. He cannot fully lift himself away from the drama of this fatal separation. Look how close the world seems, almost within reach. And when I reach, I die. The final death of his body is really the end of mediation, the end of consciousness and self-consciousness. But of course it is also the end of knowledge of the world as well. It is a drowning in the river, a leap from the bridge. And here we see why Keats is drawn towards the myth of Narcissus in the same poem:

> What first inspired a bard of old to sing
> Narcissus pining o'er the untainted spring?
> . . . And on the bank a lonely flower he spied,
> . . . Drooping its beauty o'er the watery clearness,
> to woo its own sad image into nearness."[35] (lines 163-174)

There are many attempts to re-designate Narcissus beyond the dominant Freudian version. Gaston Bachelard's challenge appears in the first chapter of *Water and Dreams, An Essay On the Imagination of Matter*. The book uses an analysis of mythic, poetic and psychological responses to water to unlock ideas of self-actualization in interactions between the imagination and various bodies of water. The first analysis of clear water quickly examines the figure of Narcissus. Rather than the hard fixed reflection of a man-made mirror "the mirror a fountain provides . . . is the opportunity of the open imagination . . . the renaturalized imagination can enter into participation with sights pertaining to river and spring."[36] Rather than just fall in love with his own image, "Narcissus receives the revelation of his identity and of his duality . . . the revelation of his reali-

---

35. Keats, 18

36. Bachelard, Gaston *Water and Dreams: An Essay on the Imaginaiton of Matter*, (Dallas: The Pegasus Foundation, 1999), 21-22.

ty and his ideality."[37] Like Keats's speaker, the reflection in the water is not about the face as much as the self being manifest in a dynamic of self and other. As with Hegel's dialectic, the "I" comes into being as a duality, needing its object otherness as foundational counterpart, here a wavery reflection of the face. Keats's ancient Bard notices the flower reflected in a pool, and sees that the pool offers the flower the chance of self-recognition. It is the bard that turns the flower into Narcissus, a reversal of the regular myth of a pining youth turning into a flower. Narcissus becomes an image of the poet as Man looks into nature to see the duality of his own nature: "But at the fountain, Narcissus has not given himself over exclusively to contemplation of himself. His own image is the center of a world . . . the whole forest is mirrored, the whole sky approaches to take cognizance of its grandiose image."[38] Bachelard reclaims Narcissus as the poetic imagination, certainly drawn to contemplate its own image, but drawn into a greater network of othernesses at the river edge; this becomes a moment when the whole universe is actualized via the engaged imagination finding itself in an opening awareness. Keats's ancient poet sees the flower's beauty as a chance for that beauty to recognize itself, "a dialectic activity between individual narcissism and cosmic narcissism."[39] We cannot embrace the value of individual vision, poetic vision if you like, if we close off the incident within a frame of mere individuality. Bachelard offers a quote by Joachim Gasquet which extends the scope to see "The world is an immense Narcissus in the act of thinking about himself."[40] The myth that often halts as a failed engagement with otherness sees instead the self as a venue for all creation (much more Blakean in scope). What Narcissus sees written on water is nothing less than the universe.

---

37. Ibid., 23
38. Ibid., 24
39. Ibid., 26
40. Ibid., 24

This is Bachelard's Narcissus of course[41], Keats's remains drugged by a sad psychology that does not fully embrace its own duality, but here and there we see that he sees it as essential.

In the end his epitaph seems to me a great joke. Against himself, with all it's cloying pseudo-self-deprecation, against the vanity of poetic immortality (his own desire for it, and others wanting it for him), against those seeking solace (or answers) by visiting his grave, and in the end against the whole notion that a grave holds anything at all. An apparently simple offering, it sets itself as a paradox, *writ in water* carved in stone (the material of one denying the meaning of the other), two elements at odds, held together and forever held apart. It has learned its lesson from Shelley's *Ozymandias*, but paradoxically, laughably, gone on to become the most resilient and famous epitaph we have.

*

Keats and Shelley share a number of sites of memorial: both are given plaques in Poets' Corner, Westminster Abbey; both also share the two sites in Rome. There is the Keats-Shelley House Museum, shouldering the Spanish Steps where Keats lived and died, though Shelley never visited. Then there is the famous Protestant cemetery, hard by the Pyramid of Cestius (though little of Shelley's earthly remains can lie there, after his funeral pyre on the Amalfi coast).

In *Adonais*, his famous elegy to Keats, Shelley encourages the reader to visit the cemetery that a year later would house his own grave.[42] In the fourth stanza Milton is also lamented, "Blind, old and lonely," and mocked by the restored Royal-

41. The successful Narcissus accepts his constitutional dialectic with something like an Hegelian *aufhebung*ing.

42. We've seen that Keats's grave echoes Beaumont and Fletcher's *Philaster*. Shelley's quotes Shakespeare's *The Tempest*:

Nothing of him that doth fade,
But doth suffer a sea change,
Into something rich and strange.

ist regime. Nonetheless unbowed in spirit he passes "unterri-fied,/Into the gulph of death."[43] What sort of gulf is death? The gulf appears to be between two mutually exclusive realms, held over and apart from each other: one of mortal life the other perhaps of immortality in the shape of poetic fame. Presum-ably the gulf hints at the grave the body is tipped into, "but his clear Sprite/Yet reigns o'er earth; the third among the sons of light."[44] Milton, having entered the gulf has risen to become a star, along side Homer and Dante. The transformation here seems to accept the emptiness of the gulf as having potential transcendental power. Unlike Keats's morbid Narcissus[45], Mil-ton has not sat on one side of the gulf staring across the abyss at the other, he has dived in "unterrified," and in so doing has been transformed into a god-like immortal, figuratively placed as a star in the heavens. So how does someone "dive" into the abyss *and* reach the other side? It seems that this bridging effect is significant of something like Hegel's *Aufhebung*. In accepting the ungrounded nature of self (the "between" of the gulph), as constituted on otherness (the other side), one enters fully into the realm of consciousness (language), becoming an immor-tal "Sprite."

This is from *Aerial's song, Act i scene ii*, which famously opens "Full Fathom Five…" addressing Ferdinand with news of his apparently drowned father. Nothing that is left will fade, because nothing that is left is physical. That which was Shelley has suffered a sea change (Shakespeare's is the first usage of "sea change" which we take to mean a significant shift). Of course he has suffered a change at the hands of the sea, but the *sea change* we are drawn towards reading is the shift from a physical being to a spiritual one. It doubles the reference to his drowning when we consider that the quote comes from *Aerial's song*, *Aerial* being one of the names of the boat which sank with him aboard.

43. *Shelley's Poetry and Prose*, eds. Reiman & Fraistat (New York: W. W. Norton, 2002), 412.

44. Ibid., 412. Milton's immortal "reign" is in contrast to own phys-ical depletion, as though the failure of his body, his blindness, leads to his becoming a source of "spiritual" light. It's also obviously held in contrast to the worldly regime of mocking Monarchists.

45. See *The English Elegy* by Peter Sacks for a lucid discussion of *Adonais* as a Narcissistic transference.

Hegel's dialectical vision culminates in the victory of the ideal, a transcendence of the apparent emptiness of the signifier, to embrace the universal. Shelley's transcendent *Adonais* enacts a similar vision of success.

The elegy itself plays out a narcissistic transformation, whereby Keats becomes Shelley, or at least Shelley takes his own part as an immortal poet, where the death of Keats becomes an example of poetic creativity, and rather than remain a sacrifice that returns annually as the name *Adonais* might suggest, Keats's poetic vision elevates him to the position of an eternal light, a star[46]. It's tempting to read Shelley's elegy simply as an allegory of Platonic transcendence (and it does indeed start out with a misattributed quote of Plato), of a dualistic vision that describes the human as "the leprous corpse touched by this spirit tender."[47] But Shelley is using the elegy to develop his own understanding of what death might mean, and what poetry's relation to death and immortality might be. The leprous corpse "exhales itself in flowers of gentle breath,"[48] the anemones of the returning Adonis, but also, the poem itself is exhalation. Such exhalations are not merely the corpse giving up its final breath, but are themselves "incarnations of the stars, when splendor is changed to fragrance."[49] Ideas, or po-

46. Something of the ambivalence of the signifier can be read in the name *Adonais*, a combination of *Adonai* and *Adonis*. *Adonis*, a figure from Greek mythology seems to have originally been one of a few annually sacrificed fertility gods, cut down young but reborn (as with all agricultural deities). In Ovid he is beloved of Aphrodite and Persephone, spending part of the year with each. He is killed by a boar, set upon him by jealous Artemis. He returns each year in the shape of an anemone, a short-lived flower whose petals were made of Adonis's blood by Aphrodite. The name Adonis shares the same root as *Adonai, Adon* meaning lord. *Adonai* is the plural form, a hint at the multiple-named nature of the Hebrew deity. So *Adonais* is both the sacrificed individual, beloved of the gods and the multi-faceted unnamed One itself. It is the before *and* after of the game of mortality.

47. Shelley, 416

48. Ibid., 416 *Anemone*, from the Greek *anemos*, wind, literally means "daughter of the wind."

49. Ibid., 416

ems, are not original to the body, but are incarnations of the eternal visited upon the body. Adonis's anemones are eternal in the same way Keats's poems are, not through their frail body, but the fragrance of the eternal that they "illumine."[50] But (as with Descartes and his pineal gland) Shelley still worries through the actual nature of this exchange. Echoing *the Nightingale*, Shelley asks whether Keats in his current state "wakes or sleeps."[51] And decides "he is not dead, he doth not sleep--/He hath awakened from the dream of life."[52] To die is to return to nature. But Shelley does not imagine that poetic genius suffers the same fate as other ephemera: "he is a portion of the loveliness/Which once he made more lovely."[53] Like a flower his blossoming made the world a lovelier place, but his blossoming had the fragrance of poetic genius, and "lofty thought lifts a young heart above its mortal lair,/and love and life contend in it . . . the dead live there."[54] The dead are his poetic forebears, they "live" in his heart. It is the fragrant idea (the poem or anemone) that shows the poet his immortal (or "dead") part. Paradoxically it is this vision, read in the works of dead poets, this dead part, this "transmitted effluence"[55] that cannot die. It cannot die because it never was mortal.

And so Shelley urges his reader to go to Rome. Not for the sights of decayed empire, hubris and decadent religion, but for Keats's grave:

> . . . till the Spirit of the spot shall lead
> Thy footsteps to a slope of green access
> Where, like an infant's smile[56], over the dead
> A light of laughing flowers along the grass is spread.[57]

---

50. Ibid., 416

51. Ibid., 421

52. Ibid., 422

53. Ibid., 423

54. Ibid., 423

55. Ibid., 424

56. William Shelley, his own son, pre-deceased Shelley and was buried close to Keats.

57. Ibid., 425

That "slope of green access", is not a physical sight alone, but "the brink"[58] of the abyss where we might contemplate the interactions of mortal and immortal being. That contemplation, the flowers, the poems are all fragile emissaries of immortal unity. Their physicality is their slightest aspect, there only to hold the fragrance of an idea of immortality. Shelley displays something like a Unitarian faith in an immortal "One."[59] All of Rome's glories are "weak"[60] and merely "transfuse"[61] this oneness. Rather than the living, the mortal giving "life" to permanent ideas, it is these permanent ideas that transfuse lifeblood to us by way of the dead, a reverse vampire image. In accepting this transfusion, this vision of the eternal, the poet accepts that his own essential nature is itself dead:

> The breath whose might I have invoked in song
> Descends on me; my spirit's bark is driven,
> Far from the shore[62]

The breath, an inhaled fragrance (from the anemones of former Adonises), is poetic inspiration, and the spirit's bark is Shelley's song, a boat much akin to Charon's, which takes the poet far from the shore of mortality towards the other bank. But this other bank is not reached by the poet in his mortal garbs, because "the massy earth and sphered skies are riven." There is a necessary otherness here, mortality (the mass of the bodied earth) and immortality (the sky) are placed, metaphorically over and against each other. Whichever horizon Shelley is sailing towards, we know the bark cannot reach the sky. Here again is the abyss that Milton leapt into. Shelley, in what he considered his finest poem, knows the journey he must take, it is an acceptance of his own trivial mortality and birth into eternal death. The light of poetic genius (Keats-Milton-Homer-Dante-Chatterton-Lucan-Adonais) is his "beacon" though in his human form

---

58. Ibid., 424
59. Ibid., 426
60. Ibid., 426
61. Ibid., 426
62. Ibid., 427

he is "borne darkly, fearfully afar." There is something of the gnostic in this dark vision. But there is also something of Hegel's acceptance of absence as the structural essence of our being.

The Pyramid of Gaius Cestius, from Views of Rome by Giovanni Battista Piranesi. 1750/59, published 1800-07. The Charles Deering Collection. Art Institute of Chicago. Used by permission.

III. A Dream of Piranesi

And grey walls moulder round, on which dull time
Feeds, like slow fire upon a hoary brand;
And one keen pyramid with wedge sublime.[63]

That sublime wedge with mouldering wall might well be a description of Piranesi's *The Pyramid of Caius Cestius* (1756), his most dramatic rendering of that monument. A tendency towards this drama is presented in his earlier reworked second version of the *The Pyramid of Caius Cestius, with the Porta S. Paolo and Adjoining Road* (1755). The first impression of 1755 is described thusly: "The foreground bears no inscription, and its apex is 3 1/8 inch from upper margin of plate," the second impression "darker lines of shading (horizontal) added in the sky along upper border, and the pyramid newly etched on a larger scale and with inscriptions on its r.side. Its apex is now only 1 ½ inches from upper margin of plate."[64] The first is a decent topographical sketch of a Roman relic. What the adjustment shows is a reworking of fact towards ideal. In the Boston Public Library collection this second stage is "juxtaposed to his later, much

---

63. Ibid., 425 After the mausolea of Augustus and Adrian, which I have already mentioned, the most remarkable ancient sepulchres at Rome are those of Caius Cestius and Cecilia Metella. The first, which stands by the Porta di S. Paolo, is a beautiful pyramid, one hundred and twenty feet high, still preserved entire, having a vaulted chamber withinside, adorned with some ancient painting, which is now almost effaced. The building is of brick, but cased with marble. This Caius Cestius had been consul, was very rich, and acted as one of the seven Epulones, who superintended the feasts of the gods, called Lectisternia, and Pervigilia. He bequeathed his whole fortune to his friend M. Agrippa, who was so generous as to give it up to the relations of the testator. —*Letter XXXII, Nice, February 28, 1765.* —*Travels through France and Italy*, Tobias Smollett

64. Hind, Arthur *Giovanni Battista Piranesi: A Critical Study* (London: The Cotswold Gallery, 1922), 48.

more theatrical version in which the foliage has been removed, inscriptions have been highlighted, and even the angle of the building has been modified . . . in doing so . . . extend[ing] the peak of the pyramid so that it threatens to break through the upper boundary of the etched plate."[65] It's in this later image that his training as an architect and set-designer meet in a version of the Romantic Sublime. Moving from mere accuracy towards a depiction of an artistic ideal, Piranesi has replaced a view with a vision.

Two elements are exaggerated for effect: the extravagant angle of the pyramid and the inscription on the side of the pyramid, which is increased in size and clarity. The drama of the etching comes from the edge of the pyramid cutting the plane of the image diagonally in half. Reaching to the very edge of the plate it reaches also the edge of physical rendering, of material possibility, and in so doing it splits the sky in two. It's almost as if the pyramid forces a bridge between earth and sky, holding the sky apart with a knife tip. The tip might almost be the engraver's burin, a suggestion that it is Piranesi's skill that acts as the medium between heaven and earth. The monument stands in full splendor next to the usual crumbling walls. The effect of this contrast is to suggest that the monument to Cestius is successful, intact, and unlike the walls, subject to the ravages of time, maybe something more than manmade.[66]

To the bottom right corner of the image is a small, disheveled figure reclining in front of the legend. The casually rendered scruff sits between topography and allegory, providing audience to the site of the Pyramid simultaneously to reading Piranesi's engraved description. Word and image inhabit the same realm suggesting Piranesi's rendering of the Pyramid is itself a monument of human making and imagining, drawing a point towards the very edge of the human imagination, pointing to a heaven beyond rendering. At the base of the Pyramid, literally in its shadow are a number of diminutive tour-

---

65. Wendorf, Richard *Piranesi's Double Ruin* (Boston: The Boston Athenæum, 2001), 10.

66. This contrast's with Thomas Hardy's poem on the subject which demotes Cestius to a bystander in its homage to Keats and Shelley.

ists searching the scene. The etching shows us a titanic Pyramid way beyond the scale and conception of these paltry figures. The Pyramid moves from merely real to ideal, from manmade to otherworldly, and the figures are left in the dark, struggling to read the mighty inscriptions beyond their reach. Piranesi offers us the only comprehensive view (verduto). Art accesses the realm of the immortal; the pyramid splits the sky.

Most famous of all is Piranesi's Carceri (Prisons) series. Here his architectural skills shift more fully from the world of bricks and mortar to the wholly imagined.

Many years ago, when I was looking over Piranesi's Antiquities of Rome, Mr. Coleridge, who was standing by, described to me a set of plates by that artist, called his Dreams, and which record the scenery of his own visions during the delirium of a fever. Some of them (I describe only from memory of Mr. Coleridge's account) represented vast Gothic halls: on the floor of which stood all sorts of engines and machinery, wheels, cables, pulleys, levers, catapults, &c. &c. expressive of enormous power put forth and resistance overcome. Creeping his way upwards, was Piranesi himself: follow the stairs a little further, and you perceive it come to a sudden abrupt termination, without any balustrade, and allowing no step onwards to him who had reached the extremity, except into the depths below. Whatever is to become of poor Piranesi, you suppose, at least, that his labours must in some way terminate here. But raise your eyes, and behold a second flight of stairs still higher: on which again Piranesi is perceived, by this time standing on the very brink of the abyss. Again elevate your eye, and a still more aerial flight of stairs is beheld: and again is poor Piranesi busy on his aspiring labours: and so on, until the unfinished stairs and Piranesi both are lost in the upper gloom of the hall.--With the same power of endless growth and self-reproduction did my architecture proceed in dreams. In the early stage of my malady, the splendours of my dreams were indeed chiefly architectural: and I beheld such pomp of cities and palaces as was never yet beheld by the waking eye, unless in the clouds.[67]

Not the *Dreams*, never before called as much, but dreams nonetheless, dreams of Piranesi, of Coleridge and of De Quincey, opium-like dreams of self-invented prisons, Vulcanic realms of improbable and sometimes impossible constructions. Here again we see that the subject is not Rome, or some other outlying empty tomb of a long-departed Senator, but instead it is the Artist, making art, in a realm of impossible proportions, finding again the self at the instant the burin scars the plate surface, marking a pit, a grave, a negative place out of which a bold line of fact will be stated. Here is an epitaph to being, and as with all Piranesi's plates, endlessly printed and reprinted so that the dream of being might be transported to all the studies and studios of European Grand Tourers, the real Rome, as it must now be seen, was invented by Piranesi as surely as it was by Virgil. Again we encounter an engraved legend of a legend of a legend as De Quincey quotes Coleridge quoting Piranesi, a description of a description of a description. If all roads lead to Rome, all roads are endless. Rome is an ideal dreamt up by poets and engravers. But then so are poets and engravers: "raise your eyes, and behold . . . Piranesi is perceived, by this time standing on the very brink of the abyss."[68]

IV. Nietzsche and the Empty Crypt

If we fall to Earth in the 20th Century, it is to an anonymous mass grave. The unimaginable machines of mankind have been aimed towards slaughter. Riches beyond nations are tuned towards destruction. The Vulcanic smithies are in full production. Hell is visited on Earth, Tartarus gapes open for the human race, the victims and the victors, of which at this stage we are all both. Only the gods can be blamed for such atroci-

---

67. De Quincey, Thomas, *Confessions of an English Opium-Eater and Other Writings* (London: Penguin Books, 2003), p78.

68. Ibid., 78

ties, but the gods are long dead, buried by science and worldly ambitions.

Or perhaps it is as Nietzsche thought it. Nietzsche's
Madman (in *The Gay Science*) and his prophet Zarathustra both
famously herald the news of the death of god. With it he pro-
claimed a new state of nihilism, a breakdown of the order of
meaning. For Nietzsche this was historical. What the death of
God signified was the re-emptying of the place of Christian
otherness, a loss of a ground upon which the drama of life and
death could play out. God was dead, Heaven was defunct.

The central event of Christian faith is the resurrection. The gospel of Mark describes Mary Magdalene, Salome
and Mary the mother of James arriving at Jesus's tomb to anoint
his body. What they find instead is a young man dressed in
white who tells them Jesus has been raised. After-sightings were
added later to the gospel, but it is upon this absence that Christian faith is based. The New Testament is the narrative of this
empty tomb, but as Robert Pogue Harrison acknowledges, "no
amount of empirical probing can penetrate the gospel's tomb,
whose emptiness remains the crux and crucible of Christian
faith."[69] The absent body of Christ is replaced by the eucharist. Because the body of Christ is missing, the faithful allow
for his transcendence from one site to everywhere through this
ritual embodiment, and wherever the eucharist is taken his
body is ritually manifested.[70] Emptiness becomes loaded with
presence: "It is an emptiness that reveals its contents, or lack
thereof, only to those who have already entered the crypt of its
sema by way of the sacraments."[71] The empty *sema* or sign paral-
lels the tomb's emptiness, "wherever Christ is, and in whatever mode he exists after the crucifixion, there is nothing left of

---

69. Harrison, 109

70. The great transformation from the pagan agricultural deity to the
Christian ritual is the absent corpse (supplanted by faith). Christ's
resurrection has no site of burial (and the surety this provides for
future crops) so can be transplanted infinitely. Signification of
the single crucifixion is transportable. The religion can become
transglobal rather than regional.

71. Ibid., 109

him here except the sign of his elsewhereness."[72] The ultimate
"elsewhereness" is Heaven. The sign of the faithful mortal is
grounded in an eternal afterlife. Christian faith depends upon
how one deciphers the empty crypt.[73]

For Nietzsche Christians are "Afterworldsmen" placing their
faith and attentions in a paradisiacal afterlife presided over
by a creator that "wanted to look away from himself, so he
created the world . . . I too once cast my deluded fancy beyond
mankind . . . [but] this God which I created was human work
and human madness, Like all gods! He was human, and only
a poor piece of man and Ego: this phantom came to me from
my own fire and ashes, that is the truth, it did not come to me
from the beyond!"[74] Those ashes he mentions are remnants of
past fires, and it is those ashes that signify our self-conscious
mortality. That mortality requires a response, and the
creation of a god is it. Zarathustra is the witness of human
history, of the founding of faiths.

> It was suffering and impotence [in the face of our in-
> evitable demise]—that created all afterworlds . . . it was
> the body despaired of the body—that touched the ulti-
> mate walls with the fingers of its deluded spirit. Believe
> me . . . it was the body that despaired of the earth—**that
> heard the belly of being speak to it**. And then it want-
> ed to get its head through the ultimate walls—over into
> the 'other world'. But that other world, that inhuman,
> dehumanized world which is a heavenly Nothing, is well
> hidden from men; and **the belly of being** does not speak
> to man, except as man.[75]

72. Ibid., 109

73. Hegel's Universal ideal was a similar grounding of his dialectic. A
nowhere that is transcendent.

74. Nietzsche, Friedrich, *Thus Spoke Zarathustra*, (London: Penguin
Books, 1961), 59.

75. Ibid., 59

The emptiness of the tomb echoes only the rumbling bellies of our body's needs and appetites. Signs are made by humans for humans, no god intercedes. Adorno praises Nietzsche's vision, and reiterates it precisely when describing the historical structure of the dialectical system of self and other:

> The system in which the sovereign mind imagined itself transfigured, has its primal history in the pre-mental, the animal life of the species. Predators got hungry, but pouncing on the prey is difficult and often dangerous . . . these impulses fuse into rage at the victim. . . . The "rational animal" with an appetite for his opponent is already fortunate enough to have a superego and must find a reason. The more completely his actions follow the law of self preservation, the less can he admit the primacy of that law to himself and to others. . . . The animal to be devoured must be evil. The sublimation of this anthropological schema extends all the way to epistemology. Idealism . . . gives unconscious sway to the ideology of the not-I, l'aurui, and finally all that reminds us of nature is inferior, so the unity of the self-preserving thought may devour it without misgivings. This justifies the principle of the thought as much as it increases the appetite. **The system is the belly turned mind** and rage is the mark of each and every idealism.[76]

Kant and Hegel are accused of aggression towards those disputing their ideals. The purity of Hegel's universal system is matched by his intolerance for alternative systems. Nietzsche's "liberating act"[77] was to articulate the connection between the self-generated rationalization of an ideal (religious faith for example) and hatred of the other "a mind that discards rationalization—its own spell—ceases by its self-reflection to be the radical evil that irks it in another."[78] Zarathustra's message was

---

76. Adorno, Theodor W. *Negative Dialectics* (New York: Continuum, 2004), 22-23

77. Ibid., 23

78. Ibid., 23

to notice not just the idealized self-preserving rationalization of religion, but to see that it grew up alongside a psychologized aggression towards dissenters. It is the failure of Christianity to behave tolerantly that gives the clue to its animal origins, and

> As soon as man finds out how the world [of truth] is fabricated solely from psychological needs, and how he has absolutely no right to it, the last form of nihilism comes into being: it includes disbelief in any metaphysical world and forbids itself any belief in a *true* world. Having reached this standpoint, one grants the reality of becoming as the only reality, forbids oneself every kind of clandestine access to afterworlds and false divinities.[79]

Here we are again nowhere, stood on nothing, before an empty crypt.

V. Decrypting Celan.

Heidegger understood Nietzsche's God as "the name for the supersensory realm of ideas and ideals, the "true world" of Platonism."[80] Nietzsche shows that this supersensory world is in fact a product of the sensory world. Platonism is an idealized hierarchy responding to the dialectical nature of being, and Religion becomes merely one act in the process of being (and for Nietzsche an act that has played out). Rather than life having lost its groundedness, "the essence of nihilism lies in history . . . then metaphysics as the history of truth of beings as such is, in its essence, nihilism. If finally, metaphysics is the historical ground of the world history that is being determined by Europe and the West, [then] that world history is . . . nihilistic."[81] The history of religion, of metaphysics and of being

---

79. Nietzsche, Friedrich *The Will to Power* (New York: Vintage books, 1968), 13.

80. Critchley, Simon *Very Little . . . Almost Nothing* (New York: Routledge, 1997), 15.

81. Heidegger, Martin *The Question Concerning Technology*, (New York: Garland, 1977), 109.

has been one of finding a ground upon which the self can place itself in (and) its dialectical schema.

If one accepts that all such groundings are tokens of psychological need where does that leave us? Nietzsche hints that only the "reality of becoming" provides us with a direction, we cannot stand on a place, we can only notice the pathway towards. For Heidegger we no longer dwell in the house of God (the Platonic realm of ideas, the absent yet Resurrected Christ) "The time of the world's night is the destitute time . . . it can no longer discern the default of God as a default. Because of this default, there fails to appear for the world the ground that grounds it."[82] Now all we have according to Nietzsche and Heidegger is "the abyss of the world that must be experienced and endured."[83]

For Heidegger any attempt to overcome nihilism oversteps the bounds of Being, denies its historical truth, and establishes a false idol, a new false ground: "the history of Being begins with the nihilation of Being, and metaphysics wants to know nothing of this nihilation, this nothing."[84] For Heidegger, then, the essence of nihilism lies in history, in the manner in which Being has fallen into nothing."[85] We cannot ignore this nihilism in moving forward.

> Thinking and poeticizing must in a certain way go back to where they have always already been and at the same time have still never built. However, we can only prepare such a dwelling in that place through building. Such a building may scarcely have in mind the erection of the house for the God or the dwelling places for mortals."[86]

---

82. Heidegger, Martin, *Poetry, Language, Thought* (New York: Perennial, 1971), 89-90.

83. Ibid., 90.

84. Ibid., 90.

85. Critchley, 17.

86. Heidegger, Martin *The Question of Being* (New York: Twayne, 1958), 103-5.

The character of our task is one of historical destiny. Heidegger knows the historical tendency to want to place ourselves, to want a ground for our being, his metaphors admit as much. In thinking and poeticizing, in using language we must find ways to acknowledge the abyss. We cannot build another temple to false idols. Neither can we reach our own mortality as it is constituted on death, our essential otherness. We have seen that the crypt is empty.

Our venture then is to endure, to be. As beings we are participants in the history of Being. "The Being of beings is the venture"[87] So our venture is to make our way towards. We do this via language, because History is language, but even more than this "Language is the precinct (templum), that is the house of Being."[88] "The whole sphere of presence is present in saying."[89]

> When we go to the well, when we go through the woods, we are always already going through the word "well," through the word "woods", even if we do not speak the words . . . Thinking our way from the temple of Being, we have an intimation of what they dare who are sometimes more daring than the Being of beings. They dare the precinct of Being. They dare language.[90]

Rather than metaphysicians Heidegger exalts poets as the most venturesome language users, those that turn towards the abyss, venturing the Open. For Heidegger the story of Being in the 20th century is a poet's story.

Paul Celan's work[91] bears witness to the atrocities of the Shoah. Or you might say he enters the German language, which

---

87. Heidegger PLT, 99.

88. Ibid., 129.

89. Ibid., 130.

90. Ibid., 129.

91. Heidegger admired Celan's work, but their meetings failed as Celan sought an explanation or at least an apology for Heidegger's involvement with the Nazi Regime that he never received.

itself "will have been a privileged witness."[92] His inhabiting of the German language then is fraught: "what is certain is that he both loved and mistrusted words to a degree that has to do with his anomalous position as a poet born in a German-speaking enclave that had been destroyed by the Germans[93]. His German could not and must not be the German of the destroyers."[94] His path must be written in the language he can never fully accept. As Pierre Joris puts it, the dilemma "involves a complex double movement—to use the terms of Empedocles—of *philotes* (love) for his mother('s tongue) and *neikos* (strife) against her murderers who are the originators and carriers of the same tongue. He is caught in this love/strife dynamic, the common baseline or ground of which (as *Grund*, ground, but also and simultaneously as *Abgrund*, abyss) is the German language, irrevocably binding the murdered and the murderer, a dynamic that structures all of Celan's thinking and writing."[95]

His fundamental dilemma[96] maintains a schism, opens up an abyss at the very heart of his work, an emotionally wrought version of the groundless nature of language. The German language becomes the arena of his engagement, but never a home. Never again a home.[97] The language of the poem becomes a nomad's dwelling, an obfuscated address that acknowledges the language's divisive past, articulates his fractured experience of being and offers a necessarily fraught way forward. His poems endure.

92. Derrida, Jacques, *Sovereignties in Question, The oetics of Paul Celan* (New York: Fordham University Press, 2005), 67

93. Paul Ancel or Antschel (Celan was an anagram adopted in 1947) was born in 1920, in Czernovitz, Bukovina. His parents were deported to an extermination camp in 1942.

94. Hamburger, Michael, *Paul Celan: Poems* New York: Persea Books, 1980), 20.

95. Joris, Pierre, *Paul Celan: Selections* (Berkeley: University of California Press, 2005), 4-5.

96. From the Greek *di*, twice and *lemma*, premise, meaning a choice between equally unfavorable alternatives.

97. A nomad in life, he settled where he was never at home, in Paris, surviving until 1970 when he drowned himself in the Seine.

Always dark and difficult, Celan denied his poems were hermetic, insisting he was out to communicate the difficulties, the dislocations and anacoluthons that were accurate to his experience. He saw them as "ways of a voice to a receptive you,"[98] This brings to mind Levinas's distinction of a voice, as distinct to an animal cry. They offer a "desperate dialogue"[99] and this dialogue is the possibility of the open future of the poem. Let us attempt that dialogue. Put a stuttering self to the face of his poem.

Todesfuge (Deathfugue) probably completed in 1944, is one of his most celebrated early poems (so celebrated he eventually refused its inclusion in more anthologies). Here is the opening stanza:

Schwarze Milch der Frühe wir trinken sie abends
wir trinken sie mittags und morgens wir trinken sie
    nachts
wir trinken und trinken
wir schaufeln ein Grab in den Lüften da liegt man nicht
    eng
Ein Mann wohnt im Haus der spielt mit den Schlangen
    der schreibt
der schreibt wenn es dunkelt nach Deutschland
dein goldenes Haar Margarete
er schreibt es und tritt vor das Haus und es blitzen die
    Sterne
er pfeift seine Rüden herbei
er pfeift seine Juden hervor läßt schaufeln ein Grab in
    der Erde
er befiehlt uns spielt auf nun zum Tanz

Black milk of daybreak we drink it at sundown
we drink it at noon in the morning we drink it at night
we drink and we drink it
we dig a grave in the breezes there one lies unconfined

---

98. Hamburger, 17.
99. Ibid., 17.

A man lives in the house he plays with the serpents he
    writes
he writes when dusk falls to Germany your golden hair
    Margarete
he writes it and steps out of doors and the stars are
    flashing
he whistles his pack out
he whistles his Jews out in earth has them dig for a grave
he commands us strike up for the dance[100]

Black milk is abhorrent. The sanctity of our first human (mammalian) exchange is turned on its head. Already, at our first feeding we are poisoned. And yet "we drink and we drink it." It is all the milk that is offered to our appetites. It is still mother, our mother tongue; our nutrition and our poison. We cannot now distinguish what time of day we are at. Like the milk, light no longer signals day; night and day are both dark, counterparts of the same nightmare.

    In drinking this foul milk, in speaking (German) we are also accepting death. More than just accepting death we are, in speaking, in writing, digging a grave. But it is not a grave in the ground. It is ungrounded. It is a grave in the breeze, the breath of speaking. To speak is to dig a grave. Obviously this is not only the ontological nature of language use, where to speak is to enter self-consciousness (and to notice in that instant our own death, and to admit rupture into ourselves, a grave in our essence), this is a language that has bidden death to millions of Jews. This is the language of murderers. But there is no ground for this grave. When a man uses language (as Heidegger calls it, lives in the "House of Being") when he writes, he plays with serpents. This is a description of the black script of writing, but it is also the nature of the writhing uncontrollable monster that language is. We can say something small, catch a word by its tail, but its meaning and purpose might wriggle free, out of our easy control. The serpent is also evil. It was there at the birth

---

100. Hamburger, 50. And I must read it in translation, another border transgressed.

of our consciousness to entice us to taste of the fruit, and once we write we are never innocent again. It is our appetite.

The final few lines show a German officer whistling his pack out, dogs perhaps, to track escapees, but no, it is Jews, his dogs, and they are called to dig graves (their own future graves). They are as anonymous as dogs in a pack. He does not use language to meet them. He does not humanize them. He whistles.

Then they are called to play music, which for the dancing Germans is entertainment, but for the Jews, the music, the same notes, these notes, is not a dance, it is a service to the Master. This one song is simultaneously a song of the master and the dog, two incompatible worlds in one, it is the German Language and it is a Death fugue. A fugue is a musical composition interweaving contrapuntal themes, that is, two aspects woven into one piece, the ambivalence that is present for Celan in using the German Language. A fugue state is a disturbed state of consciousness in which the one affected seems to perform acts in full awareness but upon recovery cannot recollect them. This describes both the victims of the concentration camp (the Jews playing the music) and the Germans themselves after the end of the war (those dancing).

None of what I have written is certain. It is a brief response, a partial reading of a short passage, but we see enough to notice that here is the work of a poet at home in and in exile from his language. The fugue state is now the human condition. The atemporality of the ordeal might suggest that once we open up the language to such atrocities the milk is black, and we drink and we repeat. We appear to know what we are saying, but we continue now on a path of mass destruction. Part of the job of reading such a poem is to notice our own buried culpability, our own part in the dance.

This poem became so ubiquitous that Celan refused to allow it to be included in future anthologies or to be read at future readings. A poem that becomes too famous runs the risk of not being encountered as anything but a celebrity. He was also "put out by the positive critical reception... for example . . . the poet Hans Egon Holthusen . . . claim[ed] . . . that Celan's poem 'escapes the bloody horror chamber of history' to 'rise to the ethereal domain of pure poetry' via a 'dreamy,' 'surreal' and 'transcendent' language."[101] The poem was being held up as an aesthetic object not a testament to suffering. School anthologies "queried the poem's formal aspects—avoiding any discussion of its explicit content."[102] The difficult dialogue was being paved over with formal rhetoric and familiarity. If semantically the poem called into question the ground of poetry, its formality hearkened back to a tradition that still held faith in the identity of a speaker and in that speaker's ability to offer a valid perspective, to bear witness. His work turned towards a stark, more stripped down form. There could be no future focus on formal beauty alone.

> Like one speaks to the stone, like
> You,
> To me from the abyss, from
> A homeland hereward, dis-
> Sister, hereward
> Thrown one, you,
> You pretime for me,
> You me in the nothing of a night,
> You in the but-night en-
> Countered one, you
> But-you—:[103]

The first stanza of *Radix Matrix*. What is this way with language? To tear it up, to stutter, and yet still to move towards speaking. Each word is tested for its authenticity, and each is found wanting. We cannot settle easily into its sense. How is this dialogue? It is dialogue rather than monologue. It is language broken open into newness. But it is a dialogue that admits itself to be across an unbridgeable gap. To speak to a stone is to admit failure, but to speak anyway, to open a dialogue in the knowledge that one will receive no answer. The "you," the reader, is like a stone to the poet. The poet too is like a stone, cannot be reached: "the you and I of the poem are caught in an

---

101. Joris, 21.

102. Ibid., 21.

103. Ibid., 83.

unending, indeterminate interchange."[104] The poem becomes a message about itself, a dialogue between its impenetrable otherness. Unlike the ancient epics that witness the establishment of a homeland, the homeland is only located in a *hereward*, a movement towards a place. *Hereward* repeats as if to emphasize that it is not a set location, it is a movement towards otherness, this poem, in effect, a dialogue, a between. It stands in the place of the place of gathering. The dialogue exists because for both the you and the I the poem is all that exists as a homeland, and it is a shared nothingness.

The poem shares a withholding: as Derrida puts it, "the possibility of a secret always remains open."[105] but for Derrida secrets are hidden in boxes. Celan "never ceased encrypting,"[106] and offers no key to the encryption, no " key to the crypt."[107] The poem remains open because it is impenetrable, because reading it cannot finish. Derrida wants to see the multiple readings we make of the encrypted language as a secret "potential energy deep in the crypt of the poem,"[108] but there is no interior of a stone. The faith needed to encounter a Celan poem is not the same faith that stares into an empty crypt and hopes for a resurrected body, the faith needed is to read knowing the crypt is always empty, and to read that emptiness as the shared otherness of being. There is no key, there is no door, there is no ground for a grave. It's an open secret.

VI. Notley breaking the code

All those white men: all that death. Alice Notley's 2011 publication *Songs and Stories of the Ghouls* carries on from her *Alma, or The Dead Women* (2006) in its visionary "voicing" of unrepresented

---

104. Ibid., 27.

105. Derrida, 67.

106. Ibid., 67.

107. Ibid., 26.

108. Ibid., 90. Placing a secret chamber inside the poem plays out a motif familiar in descriptions of mind/body dualism. The sense of language having an inner room echoes the desire to locate a soul hidden somehow within the body.

or misrepresented women. It takes up the on-going challenge of *Descent of Alette* (1996) to recast the epic as a feminist masque or choral, no longer just the story of a conquering male hero. Rather than dismantle the poem into tormented fragments like Celan, Notley rebuilds the genre as a new city. The polarity of self and other is overcome in an extensive play of multi-vocality, where form and semantics bend to allow a radical restructuring of the dialectical self, that no longer protects the I from the you, but sees the I and you as constitutional to a consciousness that takes place in a realm supported by but separate from the body: the poem.

  Songs self-consciously reclaims the stories of Dido and Medea (amongst others), challenging the cultural monuments of Virgil and Euripides (amongst others), burning the language of the conquerors to the ground and building in its place a city of ghouls, of the voices of trampled cultures, in an ongoing city poem: a "ghoulopolis."[109]

  The first chapter "Introducing Carthage" rebuilds Dido's history with a new city. "What is the name of this city? Is it really Carthage; I think that name will do for now."[110] In a way the name of the city is not important because once named it can be placed in a conventional history. By recasting the past Notley seems protected from overthrow, because the past is dead and buried, right? The past is meant to stay stable. It's our current heritage. But it's not the heritage Notley wants. Notley's chosen heritage is a hidden history of magic and female community. As she says, "I must remember a new past."[111]

  Her vision unearths a history like an archeological dig, bringing unwritten images and stories to light, from the infinite resource of "Dead," the place of ghouls. This new city houses the ghouls "millions of bodies winged ghouls is there enough space for them here as they return. . . . Do you see the small masks? Small since so many have died; and so many

---

109. Notley, Alice *Songs and Stories of the Ghouls*, (Middletown: Wesleyan University Press, 2012), 56.

110. Ibid., 9.

111. Ibid., 11.

of their words have disappeared."[112] The ghouls are broken relics "everywhere. Or are we art; or shattered cultures. Or, individual victims, lost poems, broken torsos . . . old corpses."[113] All that is left of the smashed culture of the victims is fragments. The speaker is not Notley, it is the history of the dispossessed given voice. It is the voices of these ghouls, these fragments that are everywhere underneath the dominant culture we live in now:

When I was traumatized in my sex and ceased to mate with anyone. For you will understand severe breakage of a work or cultural entity results in myriad heads stolen, small masks that might be dug up only-no temples or grand monuments. And I was repeatedly broken and possessed by scholar-archaeologists as well as starving natives and conquering soldiers.[114]

Notley's personal traumas link her to a history of the traumatized. There are no temples left, those have been destroyed, but it is impossible to destroy every trace, and the small artifacts are picked over by the dominant survivors, by scholars, who conquer the culture again by understanding and classifying the fragments (incorporating them into the dominant ideology), and by the black market (the dominant ideology!). This cultural midden is not only the war zone, but is the language itself, is Notley's own poetry.

Throughout the book Dark Ray, a figure of the establishment, engages with the work, craving access to and control of the speaker's body. Dark Ray is a coroner who tries to read the interiors of bodies in order to understand and dominate the world and work of the ghouls. His dismembering of the body is an allegory of critical dismemberment. His thinking is atomistic, and dualistic. His expectation of finding the ghoul in the body is a "ghost in the machine" fantasy. His dissection of the poetry is the same. If he can open up small passages per-

112. Ibid., 14.
113. Ibid., 33.
114. Ibid., 52.

haps he can understand it, finish it, rebury it. *Songs* has in effect already allegorized exactly what I am now doing[115].

Dark Ray's cut open Medea. Can he find what he wants?...The reason/no one will ever understand me: I don't break. It's easy for you to read a fragmentary being, shaped conceptually by you. And oh god for a short while I tried to be fragment. That means yours. Anyone's understanding of anything or foreshortens it . . . Slipped away. I always got away.[116]

Here I am fulfilling the prophecy of her text, offering a fragment by way of explanation, cutting the body to pieces to explain and make it mine. Dark Ray's (and my) version of *Songs* is an attempt at conquering through fragmentation. Dark Ray's cronies in his book club, meet to hash out poems, "the suggestion is that all bodies are full of words . . . there is a murder plot involving a club member who kills to provide the coroner with bodies for his club's eventual reading activities."[117] Notley has even written her own murder at the hands of the critic/coroner and his reading group into the poem, but the book proceeds, proof of its own indomitable independence. The book defies his "manumission," his logic, his history, "he hates the non regular nature of Dead. He just knows ancient countries can't arise and dissolve like that."[118] Surely no one can simply re-invent history. But Notley is making it happen, "I'm writing this as if I were inventing it, but it keeps getting truer and truer"[119].

Or at least the voices she hears are, because as she insists: "I'm not even making this up,"[120] which means both that she is telling the truth, but also that she is not the source. Though there seems often to be a central speaker, the poem/

115. I was once inscribed an honorary "Dead Woman" in my copy of *Alma*, but that was before I wrote this explanatory prose!

116. Ibid., 67.

117. Ibid., 40-41.

118. Ibid., 47.

119. Ibid., 38.

120. Ibid., 152.

city opens a space to house all of the dispossessed ghouls. There is no distinction between speakers, "I lived with whatever you said because I could sing it, the sources say."[121] There is no signaled ownership of the poem, it is a common ground. When *Songs* takes on the story of Medea, it doesn't just dispute the official Euripidean version, ridiculing the idea of a poisonous dress, it becomes Medea's voice, one of the trampled masks *Songs* picks up and wears: "Who is Medea if she isn't what I do now?"

And then *Songs* becomes Dido: "You are Dido, founder of a city draped in the red cloth of the individual."[122] Individuality is merely an instance of voice. The red cloth of the body is a (con)temporary host for language, but not its source (throughout the book the living eat blood sacs to feed the fleshy self), the body is not where the poem's voice originates, nor even where it lives. This is what frustrates Dark Ray in his search[123]. The voice cannot simply be killed with the body, because the poem provides another body for the voice :

> I found
> my other body—composed of a
>   poem-like
> substance,
> how what? You'd have to spend
>   a lifetime
> doing it
> out of *need*, not vanity. So
>   this other body
> This other body went forth with
>   its night-
> mare prayer.[124]

As a poet Notley has learned to access this universal place of the poem: "It has taken me 59 years to achieve/this quality of per-

---

121. Ibid., 15.

122. Ibid., 150.

123. The soul is not "in the body."

124. Ibid., 124-25.

fect desertion,"[125] to leave the flesh and enter over to "the dead world I am so alive in or/vice versa." [126] In giving herself over to the world of the poem *Songs* has become a meeting ground for the ghouls. It becomes an exemplary site of community, in stark contrast to the monumental epics of male history. The reason poetry is such a safe haven, the reason

> the ghouls speak in "poetic" language, [is]because they are souls whose stolen lives have been "prolonged" by the *poetic* within them. The only aspect of the human that hadn't been analyzed and "understood."[127]

So avoiding the conquering logic of the coroner/critic Dark Ray (and myself, and this hatchet job) becomes an essential task for *Songs*. *Songs* cannot be easily read, so as not to be controlled, filed away and stamped "understood." *Songs* isn't difficult *per se*, but the frank account of being irreducible troubles anyone wanting to "get" the book. One senses that a reading is a perspective, but not the final word. *Songs* is a station towards, and must continue to give vent to as many voices of Dead as can be heard (and Notley is in a rich vein of prolific outpouring). "So many of the dead came to me that their transparencies covered my visage,"[128] from the poem, *Millions of Us*. This is not a faith in an afterlife:

> All great religions failed . . . no unearthly afterlife, no reincarnation, no nirvana, no return as soul of tree or stone, no being transmitted into pure racial flow, nothing as simple as atheistic-type extinction. No. We're all ghouls.[129]

Songs abandons all faith-systems apart from the faith in poetry as a universal voice of the non-conqueror. True to her contrar-

---

125. Ibid., 139.
126. Ibid., 132.
127. Ibid., 145.
128. Ibid., 167.
129. Ibid., 148-49.

ian agenda, *Songs* does at times contradict its avowed opacity to "explain" itself:

> I want you to understand I can affect your physical pro-
> cess by writing. I'm not contradicting what I previously
> said: I'm not going to touch you. My hands don't stick
> out of the page; and I don't want to make you cry. I want
> to demonstrate that this—the world we live in—is imag-
> ined, and transmutable in more ways than we are used to
> discussing.[130]

She wants the reader to "understand" that the ways of understanding how the world exists are mostly misunderstood. The
world we really "live" in is not the physical material realm of
the blood-sac, but the world of the poem: "The fact that our
souls are poems is obvious, once it has been stated."[131]

And this soul doesn't really live at all. Not in the body. It
never did: "Poetry tells me I'm dead; prose pretends I'm not."[132]
Prose tries to explain, it is the engine of empire and of logic. It privileges the individual animal that bursts into self-consciousness as a language being. Poetry flies beyond us, before
we even begin to overhear its myriad voices it has been a realm

---

130. Ibid., 39. There are many theories of consciousness doing the
rounds just now, but increasingly a number that are beginning to
conceptualize the prospect of two levels of conscious behavior: animal
consciousness, brain activity (internal) and human self-consciousness
(external). Many believe this external consciousness is forged by (the
human capacity for) language. Language offers a place to reflect upon
our animal selves. It is not possible to "support" language without
our animal brains, but it is also impossible to reflect upon our animal
selves without the storage system of language. Much of what Notley
describes fits into such a theory. Consider for example Edelman
and Tononi's *A Universe of Consciousness,* especially chapter 15. Or for
a tour of historical classifications of Homo Sapiens, Agamben's *The
Open.* The ghouls are creatures of the second level of consciousness,
characters of language.

131. Ibid., 146.

132. Ibid., 39. As a counterpart to Rimbaud's "I is an other", we have
Mallarmé's "I am utterly dead" (letter to Henri Cazalis, 14 May 1867).

for centuries. Poetry is the city of voices. So the crushed and downtrodden can be rejuvenated by song. That's where these souls abide. Notley's familiarity with the ghouls is really just the self-knowledge of a languaged soul. Language is not ours. Self is language, language is otherness, otherness is selfhood.

As a woman and a poet Notley inherits the job of speaking against the "I" of the male world. Of reclaiming the I in its union with otherness. As a white man reading the book, I feel obviously aware of an ambivalent exclusion/inclusion (like a tourist dismissive of other tourists), of trespassing, but perhaps more than this I feel everyone is invited, just not as a "you." Don't come as you are, come as we are.

> I am a
> part of your
> being
>
> from before
> your
> birth; you and I
>
> know each
> other so
> well we don't have to
>
> almost
> don't have to
> do this"[133]

Notley knows that language visits her, is changed by her interactions, but does not begin with her. Nor does she have the final say. But she does have the vital task of "stripping the conquerors' word,"[134] of founding a city rather than conquering one: "I am a founder not a conqueror"[135] As an American (the

---

133. Ibid., 42.
134. Ibid., 17.
135. Ibid., 35.

silliness of the Kingdom[136]) she is the inheritor of a terrible legacy: "I Was always afraid I would kill. Americans can't get by/ without weapons."[137] *Songs* has to revise a culture sick with conquering fervor. *Songs* has to repeal the atrocities and build a city for the victims, the ghouls: "Only a/city, of so many fates/gone, unremembering presences."[138]

> Do you remember when you
> First realized people
> Were willing to kill each
> Other for almost no reason?[139]

Killing is a profound transgression misunderstanding the nature of the other in oneself. Killing is a statement of isolation, of establishing authority of the "I", often in the name of God and Country. But god and country are just more male "I"s. End points of relation, not relationships. Notley's appointed task is not about herself, her voice is many: "I write from Dead and all I'm sure of is that I continue, no matter what body I'm in."[140] *Songs* emerges from the ruins as a newly founded city. She must destroy "Rome from within the sepulcre of Carthage."[141] which means destroy the Catholic Church, destroy Virgil, destroy the all-conquering empire and its history. "I make my mind as ancient as I can to expel you. You the story." Her new history must burn Rome to the ground and replace its violence with a salving venue for the voice of otherness. A dominating culture is one which rationalizes with rhetoric towards its own ends. Hers is not self-promotion, it is self-obliteration in the task of otherness. Like Blake, her system is one of radical antinomianism, and like Blake she progresses by overcoming self in a poetics of universality: "Mine is to teach men to despise Death & to go

136. Ibid., 138.

137. Ibid., 96. What is America now but a culture of killing. Just look its annual expenditure.

138. Ibid., 193.

139. Ibid., 112.

140. Ibid., 37.

141. Ibid., 7.

on/ in fearless majesty annihilating self"[142] Physical death is the weapon of the conqueror, and fear of that death is self–preservation. But the "life" *Songs* lives is in a body of words. In her acceptance of a self-annihilation into radical otherness, Notley gives herself over to inhabit the poem and accepts her role as a ghoul. She writes a new Aeneid, offering to Virgil an alternative as radical as Blake's rewriting of Milton (and similar in that Blake felt Milton had failed on his first earthly visit due to his inability to accept his female counterpart, Ololon. It is Blake's poem *Milton* that draws Milton back from a purgatorial state, and forges the union between Milton and Ololon—I/You— that allows Milton to transcend this mundane world into eternity). By accepting her task as a carrier of language she undermines the positivistic assertions of authority and authoritarianism, she undoes the sham one-sided politics of self: "You still think you're you, tough."[143]

After millenia of wars, the history of mankind ("a frigid insult"[144]), "only words can cure us now."[145] *Songs* is not a monument for the unknown dead (women and Indians in this case) so much as a leveling of all monuments by a choir of ghouls. Monuments claim ground, and songs do not:

We have this project to change our silence into the beautiful city of a voice.[146]

142. Blake, William *Milton: A Poem* Milton Book the first, 41

143. Ibid., 151.

144. Ibid., 188.

145. Ibid., 187.

146. Ibid., 170. I must step aside from my dissection/dissertation and hand over my authority to these ghostly lyrics:

3 Herrick's Wild Civility

When one reaches for a book to take on a trip there might be any number of reasons for making a choice, but undoubtedly pre-eminent for me is company. I find that more often than not I take Herrick. And I have wondered why this is. Part of the reason is that he is at once familiar, and so I bring the familiar with me as one might a friend, but he remains somewhat enigmatic. I have been reading his *Hesperides* for longer than I care to recall, and it is not as if I haven't finished reading it so much as it seems never to have finished. Part of this is the haphazard way I read, but a lot must be laid at the feet of Herrick and his idiosyncratic book, which meanders and restarts[1], and even seems to end a good many times before it runs out of poems. Titles appear and reappear, he famously bids a solemn "farewell to sack"[2] and perhaps less famously welcomes it back thirty pages later without a hint of contradiction. He acknowledges the great (clearly in a civil war era his dedications to the King are a political statement) as well as the unknown, the historical alongside the fictional. His works wander from bawdy Anacreontics to scurrilous Martialian epigrams to heartbreaking Jonsonian elegies. It is the most inclusive of books, and the most unruly. It is delightfully disordered, and as such it remains endlessly expansive, ever open, always new. In short it is great company.

Herrick is well known today as a minor poet, a cavalier poet, one of the self-elected "sons of Ben," though now he is perhaps

---

1. The book has two titles, followed very closely by nine individual "opening" poems that all describe what the book is, where it should be read, who it is for, and four hundred pages later it "closes" still offering five or six culminating poems describing his muse, his booke, his fame and himself.

2. For Herrick poetry is sack, his intoxication, and when he raises his glass to toast his confreres, he is toasting the history of western poetry.

as often read as his master Ben Jonson, and certainly as an-
thologized. His standing is secure, though not perhaps significant compared to his abilities. Swinburne considered him "the
greatest song-writer—as surely as Shakespeare is the greatest
dramatist—ever born of English race,"[3] though he suffers now
perhaps due to the influential opinions of F.R.Leavis ("trivi-
ally charming"[4]) and T.S.Eliot who saw the "inspired frivoli-
ty" in parts but found the whole to contain "no . . . continuous conscious purpose" no "unity of underlying pattern,"[5] and
conferred upon him the title of minor poet in comparison to
Herbert whom he saw as great. Neither Leavis nor Eliot were
fools, but both obviously read with agendas significantly other
than Swinburne's. And both have had more critical influence
than the eccentric Victorian or other supporters of Herrick.
If one considers the phenomenon of the canon, with the no-
menclature and pomp of canonization that takes place, it does
seem that the lyrics of Herrick might suffer in comparison to
the grand bombast of a Milton, or even the taut personal strug-
gles of Donne[6] (or the brilliant deconstructive wit of Marvell).
The 20th century may have started as a haven for Herrick's un-
doubted charms, but it did not end as one[7]. His style is will-
fully inconsistent, his silliness is unforgiveable, his dances and

3. Preface to the *Hesperides and Noble Numbers*, ed. Alfred Pollard,
London Lawrence and Bullen, I. xi.

4. Leavis, F.R. "The line of wit" in *Revaluation*, (London: Chatto and
Windus, 1936), 10-41.

5. Eliot, T.S. "What is minor poetry" in *On Poetry and Poets* (London:
Faber and Faber, 1937), 45-47.

6. More compelling to a post-Romantic audience engaged in pro
tracted self-scrutiny.

7. This is of course no place to risk a description of 20th century
poetry, but if one looks at the shift from Victorian verse through
Modernism, and the advent of Free Verse, one can see that the status
of songs as poetry has much declined, and that the merit of joy and of
the delightful has been relegated as well. Disjunction often feels more
appropriate. Beauty seems to embarrassingly ignore catastrophes and
international tragedies.

frills, even his playful seductions seem hopelessly naïve and out of keeping with modern life, as outdated as the festivals and countryside idylls he describes. But perhaps it was always so. And Herrick is not as frivolous in his lyricism as it might appear. He is crafty, that is, he is an exquisite craftsman, something that the son of a goldsmith, and a trained goldsmith himself, would have seen as the highest compliment, but he is also crafty. His message is subtle, as subtle as it needed to be in a time of great political unrest. And his task, in creating the most simple of lyrics is to continue a craft that he sees as being as vital to culture and country as it is to soul and man.

The title *Hesperides* refers to both the nymph daughters of Hesperus (the evening star Venus) and the garden they protect. The garden is the orchard of Hera, where the nymphs protect her wedding gift from Gaia, a tree bearing golden apples. Speculations as to the whereabouts of the garden vary, though it seems the location is often "to the west", giving the position the poignancy of the setting sun (think of the end of the Monarchy as the sun going down). The garden brings echoes of Eden and Elysium, and might also reflect Herrick's own status as an "exiled Ovid" in the west county of Devon. The rest of the title, "or THE WORKS both Humane and Divine" purports to offer a translation, so that we see *Hesperides* as a collection of the poetical fruits of Herrick's labours. The title conflates the work with the guarding of that work, seeing the task of poetry as both making the work and jealously guarding a divine gift. It's important to remember that Herrick is both the creator and the custodian.

Entitling the book "the Works" also hints at a posthumous collection[1], further endorse by the frontispiece portrait, an etching of Herrick as a funeral bust. The message is that herein lies the worthy remains of our author, his best part. This reading is endorsed by an epigram of Ovid "Effugient avidos Carmina nostra Rogos," ("our songs will escape the greedy funeral

---

1. Only Samuel Daniel (1601) and Ben Jonson (1616) had previously used the name for a collection of poems whilst alive.

pyres") which is actually a very obvious misquote: Ovid's original using *sola* instead of *nostra* (most early modern editions used the imperfect "effugient," *will*, rather than the modern preference for "defugient," *do*) in his elegy for Tibullus, where his implication is the subtly different "Defugient avidos carmina sola rogos"[2] ("song alone escapes the greedy funeral pyre"). Herrick's inclusivity highlights the communality of the poetic garden, seeing his own task as guardian as well as practitioner. The songs are "ours" not simply "his." He allies himself with Ovid, and thus with Tibullus, which along side the funeral bust, show his poems stretching beyond his mortal span, reaching backwards and forwards in history. This suggests *Hesperides* is an atemporal realm, a poetic Elysium or garden where Herrick and Ovid and Tibullus (as well as his beloved Jonson) can meet to drink heady inspiration from the muse's cup. Herrick's modesty (compared to Jonson's virile self-promotion, or Milton's self-appointed grandeur) is nonetheless a conscious self-election to the pantheon.

So let's look at one of his most popular lyrics, here in full:

> A SWEET disorder in the dress
> Kindles in clothes a wantonness :
> A lawn about the shoulders thrown
> Into a fine distraction :
> An erring lace which here and there
> Enthrals the crimson stomacher :
> A cuff neglectful, and thereby
> Ribbons to flow confusedly :
> A winning wave (deserving note)
> In the tempestuous petticoat :
> A careless shoe-string, in whose tie
> I see a wild civility :
> Do more bewitch me than when art
> Is too precise in every part.[3]

2. Ovid *Heroides and Amores* ed. Grant Showerman (Cambridge: Loeb 1963), 482

3. *The Poetical Works of Robert Herrick* ed. L. C. Martin (Oxford: Oxford University Press, 1956), 28

Delight is a pretty 14-line sonnet of rhyming couplets in regular iambic tetrameter, with each line a complete clause. The meter offers only one "distraction," which must be pulled out of its usual three syllables, "dis-trac-tion," into an unusual four "dis-tract-i-on" instead—something of a playful tugging of the word that might prepare us for the erring lace to follow. As is typical of Herrick there is plenty of alliteration (**d**isorder, **d**ress; **k**indles, **c**lothes; **w**inning **w**ave) and a great deal of consonance and assonance ("A la<u>wn</u> ab<u>ou</u>t the sh<u>ou</u>lders thr<u>ow</u>n"), with the syllable "in" playing a strong role in holding the whole piece together sonically and visually. Until the final "Do," each couplet begins with either the article "a" or "an," with four of the following lines beginning with an "in" or "en" sound, and the other lines at least echoing the "I" sound. Until the final rhyme of "art" and "part" Herrick rhymes a single-syllable word with a three-syllable word (or in one case "thereby" with "confusedly": a two-syllable word with a four). This masculine/feminine rhyme scheme has a ravishing effect, producing a sense of effortless flourish at the end of each couplet, almost as if we see the modest single syllable unfurl into extravagance: "dress" becomes "wantonness." Throughout, the idea of the ribbon or the lace unraveling becomes the play of the syllables, the "es" of "dress" and "wantonness" reappears in "de**s**erving" and weaves into "tempe**s**tuous," and through "carele**s**s" where the "es" becomes "s" and continues through the "shoe-string," "see" and "civility." Every "part" rhymes *art*fully, "ribbon" finds kinship in proximity to "winning," (with the central doubling of consonants) and "enthralls," where the "on" off rhymes with the "en". The play of the whole is at once seemingly effortless and intricately precise; the dress of the lover is at once disheveled, and at the same time precisely arranged as such. And as such the poem is an ars poetica. The poem is itself a reframing of a Jonson lyric:

> Still to be neat, still to be dressed,
> As you were going to a feast;
> Still to be powdered, still perfumed:
> Lady, it is to be presumed,
> Though art's hid causes are not found,

All is not sweet, all is not sound.
Give me a look, give me a face
That makes simplicity a grace;
Robes loosely flowing, hair as free:
Such sweet neglect more taketh me,
Than all the adulteries of art:
They strike mine eyes, but not my heart.[4]

Both poems shift from a description of a preference for the way a lover might dress to make a declaration on art. The mention of "art" in Jonson appears as the art of seduction, over-played by a woman too obvious in her decoration. But Jonson's references to "grace" as well as "art," in a poem about revealing the truth in small details, flags an underlying message. A longer, more showy treatise on his declared preference for simplicity in art would be counter intuitive. Both poems seduce by understatement. Both are deceptively simple. And both lyrics deceive if we under read them. They are, in that, somewhat paradoxical: they argue for simplicity while embodying a hidden subtlety. Jonson's paradox of "sweet neglect" is not as strident as Herrick's "wild civility", but both offer a clue to a shared ideology.

In his treatise *Orator* Cicero outlines the true "Attic" style, which is restrained and plain. Indeed, "the audience . . . are sure they can speak in that fashion."[5] Here we see a description of the ideal style that rhymes with Jonson's apparent simplicity. But Cicero continues in language that seems even more reminiscent of Herrick when he suggests that speech should "be loose but not rambling; so that it may be seen to move freely but not to wander without restraint."[6] The ribbons and stomacher offer just such a freedom and restraint in Herrick's *Delight*. The restraint is both linguistic and moral: "For the short and concise clauses must not be handled carelessly, but there is such a thing even as careful negligence." Cicero's "careful neg-

---

4. Jonson, Ben *Complete Poems* (London: Penguin 1988), 291
5. Cicero, *Brutus Orator* (Cambridge: Loeb 1971), 363.
6. Ibid., 363.

ligence" is Jonson's "sweet neglect" and Herrick's "wild civility."
But even more telling is Cicero's supporting example for this
paradoxical neglect: "Just as some women are said to be hand-
some when unadorned—this very lack or ornament becomes
them—so this plain style gives pleasure even when unembel-
lished."[7] The precedent is well established then to see plain
style in language exemplified with a description of a woman's
clothing. And of course there are echoes elsewhere, such as
Ovid's *Amore, xiv* where he describes his waking lover: "tum quo-
que erat neclecta decens, ut Threcia Bacche."[8] ('even then, in
her neglect, she was comely, like a Thracian Bacchante.") The
image of the woman appearing to her lover in dishabille allows
for her subtle awareness at being noticed. Cicero's audience is
led to feel the oration is artless, just as the lover is led to believe the woman's look is unself-conscious. The truth is they
are artful, without being artificial. The paradox of "neglecta
decens" is more natural than any artificial make up, "imitating
that orderly disorder, which is common in nature."[9] The artifice in Herrick and Jonson is to produce plain seeming lyrics
that address the simple natural beauty of nature and women,
but are in fact supremely crafted. Herrick's *Delight* is itself exemplary of his "wild civility," an idea he repeats throughout the
Hesperides in "To Musick, to becalme a sweet-sick-youth,"[10] "Art
above Nature, to Julia,"[11] and "What kind of Mistresse he would
have."[12] Three of the four poems refer directly to the dress and
habits of his lovers, although lovers in Herrick are always idealized figures, possibly the muse and clearly offered as literary
tropes. "Wild civility" describes the art by which a lover dress-

---

7. Ibid., 363.

8. Ovid, *Heroides and Amores,* ed. Grant Showerman (Cambridge: Loeb
1963), 372

9. Jonson, Ben *Masque of Blacknesse*, 1.

10. "Lost in the civill Wildernesse of sleep" (Herrick Works), 99.

11. "Next, when those Lawnie Filmes I see/Play with a wild
civility," 202

12. "Be she shewing in her dresse,/Like a civill Wildernesse," 232

es (and undresses) and at the same time it describes the way an ideal poem might be fashioned.

Of course the concept of "wild civility" is more than classical rhetoric, and the image of a loosely dressed lover appeals to a non-puritanical age, hearkening back to a time before the regime under which Herrick is writing. *Delight* obviously echoes Jonson, and looks to the time of the Monarchy, nostalgically revisioning the period as a Golden Age. But the Golden Age is a pastoral convention, a literary device, more than it is any historical period. The tone of the book is often nostalgic, but more often than not the events seem to be literary as much as historical, and the convivial symposiastic references bring Anacreon to life for an evening of drink, as vividly as they bring Jonson back from the dead to inhabit the Apollo Room. The implication of the *Hesperides* as a posthumous work seems to suggest that more has been lost with the civil war than the King. A link to the court is cut off and poets such as Herrick are now in exile, a fate akin to death. We have a version of the fall of Rome, here and now in England. And it is up to Herrick (the pre-eminent disciple of Jonson) to provide a place, a garden, where poets may still meet. *Hesperides* is such a meeting place, where Herrick and his poetic forebears mingle and exchange.

As we have seen *Hesperides* is filled with homages to Ovid and Jonson, with allusions to and imitations of poets classical and contemporaneous. Herrick's imitations are not merely exercises of a minor poetaster. The idea of imitation acknowledges the rhetorical teachings of Cicero and Dionysius of Halicarnassus,[13] but more than that it is an instant of recitation and resuscitation. Ovid lives because we read him. Jonson lives in the vivid plain English lines of his songs. Herrick's style is self-consciously imitative, not out of failure of imagination, but out of overwhelming gratitude and humility. But one should not imagine for one minute that Herrick's poems are shallow copies, anymore than one should imagine Leonar-

---

13. Another rhetorician supporting the claims of plain style and of "art. . . concealed beneath the semblance of artlessness." *De Lysias* I.16

do's sketches from Verrocchio limited his own artistic endeavors. All poetry is a balance of imitation and imaginative deviation, or if you prefer a balance between rules and unruliness. It must in someway resemble previous poetry to be read as such. It must differ to be seen as worthy of the title. All poetry moves between these poles, Herrick's "civility" is surely his classical education. His "wildness" is that which breathes freshness and inspiration into and out of the work of his forebears to make his own. Poetry's space is the gap between the paradox of "wild" and "civil." When Horace describes his poet in Ode xxxiv: "Parcus deorum cultor et infrequens,/insanientis dum sapientiae"[14] ("I, a chary and infrequent worshipper of the gods, what time I wandered, the votary of a foolish wisdom.") it is a poet Herrick would recognize. His own "wild civility" is such a "foolish wisdom." It is at once learned and lived. His art is crafty in its artlessness, but his peasant dances are as graceful as any courtly masque.

One could argue that for Herrick the passing of the Monarchy, and the passing of courtly patronage must have seemed like the end of a very natural poetic heritage. The pastoral convention of shepherds exchanging songs was perhaps a courtly reality, and certainly it appears Herrick felt part of such an exchange with Jonson and his legendary gatherings. What seems more important in a way is not his purported Royalist leanings (*Hesperides* contains plenty of ambivalence in terms of the political dedicatees, from the King and Royalist friends to powerful Parlimentarians, none of the poems seeming to beg for political favours in the way one might expect) but his desire to preserve a poetic lineage. He needed a realm where just inheritance might survive untrammeled. But the crown is of laurels not of gold. And the realm is a poetic Elysium, not Whitehall.

Hesperides is deliberate in its political and poetical unruliness. Unlike the works of many of his contemporaries it holds no obvious political agenda, nor one single poetical style. The gar-

---

14. Horace *Odes and Epodes* ed. C.E.Bennett (Cambridge: Loeb 1968), 90.

den[15] he builds is as welcoming as a peasant's dwelling in an Arcadian grove. But with that it is a model of the ultimate poetic demense. One might argue that his model is a Jonsonian country estate with all its self-affirming grandeur and social order, or even that it is a mythical retreat, a walled garden to keep his Monarch safe. And perhaps these are more likely than a realm unfettered by such political ramifications. But these assertions are not the thorough being of the book, and there remains much delight in the disorderly *Hesperides*, in its "wild civility". The fact that he is still read, still chosen for company shows that he might well outlive more than one or two shifts in political fashion, whether it be Puritanical or Modernist.

If *Hesperides* is a princely domain, its rule is poetry, and its apples hang for generational succor. One never reaches the wall of the estate (or book's covers) with a sense of having walked the whole plot. Its companionability lies is its endless array of silly or grand features; if it is a pleasure garden, it is one so vast and various (yet intimate) as to mimic the world beyond, and when one is done with reading such pleasures, one is done with reading poetry.

Works Cited

Cicero. *Brutus Orator.* Cambridge: Loeb 1971.

Eliot, T.S. "What Is Minor Poetry?" In *On Poetry and Poets.* London: Faber and Faber, 1957.

Dionysius of Halicarnassus, *Lysias.* New York: G. P. Putnam's, 1930. Internet Archive: http://archive.org/stream/lysiaslamb00lysiuoft/lysiaslamb00lysiuoft_djvu.txt

Herrick, Robert. *The Poetical Works of Robert Herrick.* Edited by L. C. Martin. Oxford: Oxford University Press, 1956.

—. *Hesperides and Noble Numbers.* Edited by Alfred Pollard. London: Lawrence and Bullen, 1898.

Horace. *Odes and Epodes.* Edited by C. E. Bennett. Cambridge: Loeb, 1968.

---

15. And it is a very English garden in the style of William Kent or Charles Bridgeman, appearing at once natural and cultivated.

Jonson, Ben. *Complete Poems*. London: Penguin 1988.

—. *Ben Jonson's Plays and Masques*. Edited by Richard L. Harp. New York: W. W. Norton, 2001.

Leavis, F. R. "The Line of Wit." In *Revaluation: Tradition and Development in English Poetry*. London: Chatto and Windus, 1936.

Ovid. *Heroides and Amores*. Edited by Grant Showerman. Cambridge: Loeb, 1963.

Postscript: On Sublimity

*The invisibility and intangibility of that which moves us remained
an unfathomable mystery.*

—W. G. Sebald, The Rings of Saturn

W. G. Sebald arrives at the above articulation immediately
after a description of a stay in hospital, a convalescence
of the sort spoken rarely of these days. Indeed it appears now
that such convalescences are the stuff of fiction, found only in
the novels of Thomas Mann, or perhaps Denton Welch. And
it might be true to say that one remaining resort that offers us
the thoughtful and reparative time we so much need for convalescence, the time necessary to reflect upon or make meaning of the strange phenomenon of being, is in literature itself.
Sebald's description of his character's convalescence is itself a
metaphorical description of his own practice as a reader and
writer, and of the quiet solitary activity that such endeavors require. These moments of reading and writing are at once moments both of the world, but also necessarily removed from the
world. His life in the world is the life of a literary observer. His
book is littered with stories of similar folk, with those liter-
ary-minded figures that are somehow captivated by an activity
that attempts to make sense of the world whilst simultaneously
forcing their withdrawal from it. It is as if we can only take the
time to think of life when we cease to live it.

In the quote I have used, Sebald is describing an instant of watching out of a window as a passing vapour trail in-
dicates the presence of a passenger jet, high over head, filled
with its unknown population. It is so far removed from his own
circumstance that all he has access to is the evidence of its having passed. It is something of a ghost. In a way this single trail,
which reappears in his novel again a hundred and sixty three
pages later, almost a ghost of a ghost at that stage, becomes one
of many motifs that indicate the observer's distance from the
world of events. The world is held away from the observer, as if
the very act of observation forces at once an irreparable sepa-

ration that we now begin to notice almost as much as the thing we wanted to observe. It is as if all we can do is read ledgers and histories in an attempt to understand what has happened, even in our own lives. It is as if all that we have as proof of the soul's travails is the words that are left us, the trails drawn in the skies as it were. But even these are presented to us as fragments only, glimpses and ghosts, buried remains and vapours.

And I have a small confession. The Sebald epigraph that opens this essay is only a fragment of his original sentence. It continues (and indeed I purposefully cut it in half for my own purposes as all writers do with the texts of others, quoting, misquoting, dragging into new contexts) and combines his own moment of worldly reflection upon a mystery observed through a window, with a speculation on a literary predecessor who for Sebald holds a distinct fascination and with whom he holds a common burden of interest (and for whom a vapour trail, he surmises, would also be a mystery)—his sentence continues:

> for Thomas Browne too, who saw our world as no more than a shadow image of another far beyond. In his thinking and writing he therefore sought to look upon earthly existence from the things that were closest to him to the spheres of the universe, with the eye of an outsider, one might even say of the creator. His only means of achieving the sublime heights that this endeavour required was a parlous loftiness in his language. (18-19)

Sebald is talking of himself when he speaks of Browne. That is, his description of Browne is a self-portrait. He is describing his own artistic aims and his own sentences. The "parlous loftiness" he uses to describe Browne is itself a perfect example of parlous loftiness. So, what is this notion of loftiness that Sebald draws our attention to? What does he mean by using this metaphor of flight? Sebald continues to describe how he reads Browne:

> [B]ecause of the immense weight of the impediments he is carrying [the weight of erudition as well as the verbiage

of his extraordinarily long sentences], Browne's writing can be held back by the force of gravitation, but when he does succeed in rising higher and higher through the circles of his spiraling prose, borne aloft like a glider on warm currents of air, even today the reader is overcome by a sense of levitation. (19)

It seems that Sebald is describing a style of writing that affects the reader with an almost physical sensation of lifting. We know well enough that the printed word is materially bound to the earth. But we also know that language itself, especially poetic language, can aim at sublimity. It is as if the way certain *sublime* writers combine words in relation points us beyond the page, acknowledges some higher realm, provokes a desire to reach elsewhere, providing a momentum from the written ambition to the reader's own sensation.

Longinus is perhaps our first rhetorician to supply a document examining the notion of the written sublime. In the fragmentary remnants of his well-known treatise *On the Sublime* we are treated to a catalogue of tropes present in all great works along with the pitfalls that mark all literature that misses the mark for one reason or another. The great literary work remains difficult to characterize, other than to say that "by some innate power the true sublime uplifts our souls" (Longinus 107). The metaphor of elevation cannot be said to find its source here, but we can see that Sebald is reciting an immemorial ideal. And Sebald's metaphor of Browne's writing somehow over-coming gravity is here echoed by the idea of the great work having enough power to lift us up. The idea of flight and the effects of great literature are at least metaphorically cousin-germain.

During his life as a painter and an illustrator Paul Nash was frequently reminded of a recurring dreamlike desire for flight. In his wonderful short memoir *Aerial Flowers*, produced as a limited edition in 1947, Nash discusses his desire "in common with many other human creatures, I have always been more or less attracted to the idea of being able to fly." (AF 2). He never simply attributes this to a desire to be airbourne merely, but to have the freedom to fly at one's own volition. The desire was never an obsession as such, but early drawings record the act, including creatures invented that were capable of the flight he imagined and dreamt for himself. During the war he drew shocking depictions of No Man's Land, and during these studies he made tentative experiments in abstraction:

> I began, for instance, to explore in depth by new methods to re-value colour relationships and practise with more subtlety the acute problems of poise. I realize now that these were actually my first attempts to fly.

This simple, almost flat, statement is really quite stunning in its apparent awareness of what painting, that essentially flat medium, is attempting to do in the deliberate juxta-position of colours. The task of abstract painting is thus described as attempting almost the same "parlous loftiness" Sebald attributes to Browne. The material of Art points towards an immateriality. When I read this quote of Nash's for the first time I immediately thought of how this might also describe the ambitions of the written, and of poetry in particular. This was even before I had read his next paragraph:

> A few years later in the course of making a series of drawings to illustrate Sir Thomas Browne's *Urne Buriall*, I came upon the sentence referring to the soul visiting the Mansions of the Dead. This idea stirred my imagination deeply. I could see the emblem of the soul—a little winged creature, perhaps not unlike the ghost moth—perched upon the airy habitations of the skies which in their turn sailed and swung from cloud to cloud and then into space once more. It did not occur to me for a moment that the Mansions of the Dead could be situated anywhere but in the sky . . . the importance of this particular opportunity was that it afforded a further adventure in flight (AF 5).

It is as if Nash and Sebald were both elevated by exactly the same text in exactly the same way. They are both brought, sep-

arately, to similar revelations. It is the revelation of the soul
transcending the body.

Such a revelation depends upon a certain construction
of our physical and spiritual make-up, a metaphorical description that we inherit from a particular cultural and historical
context. And it might be that in our twenty-first century context this dualistic, one might say, Cartesian, construction ought
to come under some pressure. But for my interest I am not ask-
ing for my reader to image the soul and the body as clearly distinct, I am in fact looking at the moment that Browne, Sebald
and Nash notice as a kind of moment of crisis in the identity of
being. For if language is of the earth, in its poetic moments it
might be said to point to that which is beyond its own materiality, just as in moments of deep reflection the mind might become aware of a state of being that hints at a bodiless elevation.

Poetry is made of the earth. It has materiality. Indeed,
it has been the necessary project of some important twentieth
century writers to remind us of this. But it does, as does all language, point to that which is absent. In so doing it potentially
gives a model of divine ascendance. It points up. This is, you
understand, only one way to read what might take place. I offer Sebald and Nash as test cases in an inadequate study in the
phenomenon, perhaps with the same intent that James offers
examples of religious experience. What interests me is the lon-
gevity of this metaphor of transcendence, coupled with the coincidence of two readers of Browne describing their physical
response in such similar terms. Not all language is Sublime.
The task of the writer of sublimity is to find a physical pattern suggestive of such transcendence. It must remind us of the
strange and uncanny matter that it reaches for. It must reach.
It must leap, and in leaping it becomes poetry rather than just
a utile communication. Poetry is the instant of language getting
above itself. The instant of the poetic is like Sebald's instant of
the convalescent observer who sees both himself and his world,
who knows they are at once the same and separate. It is then
possible to imagine that the loftiness of poetry is its ability to
point beyond its own materiality. But the pointing is a function of its materiality. So it is not strictly dualistic. It is possi-

ble that the idea of the soul, and thus the soul itself, comes into being the moment the body notices its own self in all its limited glory. This is the moment of becoming, the mirror stage, the eating of the apple, figure it in whatever system you please. In the same way poetry comes into the poem at those instances where the poem is stretched to the limits of its body. Poetry inhabits the poem the way the soul inhabits the body (and I deliberately use terms that are old-fashioned and burdened by history, because the phenomenon of poetry is not new, just as the phenomenon of being is not). Poetry is not easy to point at even in a successful poem. It is the vaporous glimpse of the instant of the soul's departing, through the openings that yawn briefly in the imaginative thrum of the written. Poetry is the closest the body gets to touching the soul. This is because it is also the instant of the invention of that soul. It is the resort of living outside of life, it is the Mansion of the Dead, it is the realm between. All of these descriptions remain allusive rather than conclusive, because "The invisibility and intangibility of that which moves us remained an unfathomable mystery" (Sebald, 18-19).

Works Cited

Aristotle/Horace/Longinus. *Classical Literary Criticism*. New York: Penguin Books, 1965.

Nash, Paul. *Aerial Flowers*. Oxford: Counterpoint Publications, 1947.

Sebald, W. G. *The Rings of Saturn*. New York: New Directions, 1999.

About the Author

Martin Corless-Smith was born and raised in Worcestershire, United Kingdom. He has a BA and MFA in painting and print-making as well as an MFA in Poetry from the Iowa Writers' Workshop and a PhD in Creative writing from the University of Utah. He has published seven collections of poetry, most recently *The Fool & The Bee* (Shearsman, UK 2018), a novel, *This Fatal Looking Glass* (SplitLevel Press, 2015) and a translation, *Odious Horizons: Some Versions of Horace* (Miami University Press, 2019). He is currently working on translating contemporary Italian poetry. He writes, paints, and teaches in Boise, Idaho, where he lives with his partner and her dogs, cats, parrots, and children.

www.ingramcontent.com/pod-product-compliance
Lightning Source LLC
Chambersburg PA
CBHW021508090426

42739CB00007B/520